THE GREAT BLUE HERON

Library of Congress Cataloging-in-Publication Data

Allen, Hayward.
    The great blue heron / by Hayward Allen.
        p.   cm. – (Camp & cottage collection. Wildlife)
    Includes bibliographical references.
    ISBN 1-55971-094-2 : $ 16.95
    1. Great blue heron.   I. Title.   II. Series.
QL696.C52A44   1991
598' .34–dc20   91-2400
                                                  CIP

©1991 NorthWord Press, Inc.
Box 1360, Minocqua, WI 54548

Designed by Mary A. Shafer
Typeset by Lambert Desktop Publishing Service
Cover Photograph by Scott Nielsen
ISBN 1-55971-094-2

Printed and bound in Singapore

For a free catalog describing NorthWord's line of nature
books and gifts, call 1-800-336-5666.

THE GREAT BLUE HERON

By
Hayward Allen

NorthWord
PRESS, INC

Box 1360, Minocqua, WI 54548

Contents

Introduction

Slender, steel-grey, standing stationary, at first glance the great blue heron is almost invisible. Many writers use the word "sentinel" to describe their initial impressions of this impressive bird, perhaps reminded of the impassive, great-hatted guards who stand before Buckingham Palace. This immobility of the great blue heron is an illusion. What we are witnessing is a slow motion stealthy hunt for food. If the great blue heron is guarding anything, it is its territory of patrol.

The great blue is a suspicious and cautious creature, but today it has few enemies. The mature bird usually has only the bored hunter or the untutored boy with a gun to fear. The canoeist, the wading fisherman, or the waterskier rarely get close enough to count the crest feathers on a great blue heron's head. With a great "kwaaark!" the lanky bird unfurls its enormous wings and with two powerful pulls is airborne just about the time the visitor has seen the great blue.

We should remember that the resilience of the heron family is a key to the great blue's success as a species. Only a few birds, such

---

OPENING SPREAD — *There is no mistaking the graceful curved neck of a great blue heron in flight.* Photo by Stephen Kirkpatrick

PAGE 6 — *The regal profile and shining golden eye of the stately great blue.* Photo by Lynn M. Stone

OPPOSITE — *Strolling and trolling the shallows at dawn.* Photo by Lynn M. Stone

INTRODUCTION

as the passenger pigeon, have been hunted to extinction by mankind. But one hundred years ago, we came very, very close to removing the most impressive members of the family—the egret, the white and great blue herons—from the species list.

The vanity of fashion was the culprit. When it was the Day of the Plume, during the latter years of the 19th century and the early days of the 20th, the plumage of these birds became a popular fashion statement. Ladies' hats and soldiers' decorative helmets were festooned with the feathers of the most striking members of the heron family.

In 1903, bird hunters were paid $32 an ounce for plumes. It required the deaths of four herons or egrets to total one ounce. At one single London auction in 1902, 3,000 pounds were sold to haberdashers—a quick bit of multiplication reveals that 192,000 birds were killed to yield 48,000 ounces of their plumage. There are estimates that go as high as 20 million birds of 40 odd species that were sacrificed at the altar of high fashion.

Although the birds died for vanity, it could be said that they did not die in vain. The public outcry might have been slow at first, but once the legislators began to recognize the feelings of many of their constituents, laws began to be written in the first decade of this century to protect these endangered birds. It is also important to note that both the British Royal Society for the Protection of Birds and the U.S. Audubon Society were formed specifically as a result of people's need to stop the slaughter of herons and egrets.

Let us meet this remarkable and beautiful bird.

OPPOSITE — *Silhouetted against soft, sunrise ripples, a great blue waits on a piling to spot its breakfast. Photo by Lynn M. Stone*

Meet The Great Blue

"Look on the one that stands near the margin of the pure stream. See his reflection as it were into the smooth water. How calm, how silent, how grand is the scene. You might imagine what you see to be the statue of a bird, so motionless it is."

John James Audubon (1785-1851) thought the great blue heron to be one of our hemisphere's stateliest birds. When he published his landmark **Birds of America** more than 160 years ago, his portrait of *ardea herodias* was not only complete with anecdotes and ornithological information but also a magnificent print of his painting of the bird.

People have long had their own names for the great blue heron. In Audubon's day it was called an "Indian hen" or "Indian pullet," as well as "blue crane" or just plain "crane," (as it still is called in many places) or "Blue Cranky," "Poor Joe," and "Long John." The thought that the great blue might be as tasty as a chicken amused Audubon. While the very young did possess a certain tenderness, the mature bird was "not to my taste. I would prefer a crow or eagle."

When early man began prowling the edges of glaciers during the Pleistocene Age about two million years ago, he saw herons along the shores of the lakes and rivers. By then the heron family had already been around for about fifty million years, along with other birds that emerged during the Paleocene and Eocene Ages, such as cranes, ducks, pelicans and owls.

OPPOSITE — *Beware the stiff-necked great blue on the prowl.* Photo by Scott Nielsen

MEET THE GREAT BLUE

Still, *Ardea herodias* doesn't belong to the oldest orders of the earth's birds. It is only about half as old as the loon, for example, as seen in the fossil of the *hesperonis*, or the fossilized *ichthronis*, which resembles our terns. There are few good fossil remains of most birds, and for good reason: their hollow bones and feathered bodies vanished before the fossilizing conditions were affected.

So we don't know for sure how many different kinds of birds have existed in prehistoric times. One antique ornithologist, Brodkorb, estimates that there have been more than 150,000 different species of birds. Today there are only 9,000, which have been divided into 27 orders of 160 families. It has been conjectured that today there are more than 100 billion individual birds living around the globe, in every kind of habitat.

The great blue heron is one of 120 of those species that are called "long-legged waders," and among them are the classical ibis, the legendary stork, and the *ardea* family of herons. They are what is called a "colonial" bird, meaning that they tend to live in groups of significant numbers. While we usually see them as solitary waders on our various shores, they return daily in the nesting season to the colonies to tend to domestic duties.

While they might be classified according to their wading "equipment," what really characterizes these birds is their specific hunting device: their long bills. These can be as pointed as a spear, as are heron bills, or in the shape of a spoon like the spoonbills; they can be long but turn up or turn down; some are shaped like a sickle, and others have bills that look like one of Charlie Chaplin's shoes. So it can be difficult to classify these

MEET THE GREAT BLUE

birds using only one feature of their anatomy.

For centuries, for example, no one knew exactly where to put the flamingo with its peculiarly shaped bill serving as a strainer as the bird grazes through shallow, muddy water. However, one interesting, recent discovery in the 1970s—thanks to the advent of cellular chemistry—has revealed that the flamingo belongs to the same family as the stork.

So, it is the family that counts in ornithological cataloging, not just how the birds "look." The crane is considered a marsh bird, part of the order of *gruiformes*, which has 12 families and 209 species. The heron is in the order of *ciconiiformes*, and is classified as a wading bird, one of six families and 122 living species. There is some controversy, however, in this classification for there are ornithologists who do not think that *ciconiiformes* is a natural "order." In fact, the Smithsonian's Storrs Olson has written that this classification is "a totally artificial assemblage of long-legged, desmoguathous water birds having little in common." This school of thought places the heron family as merely a radiation of the *gruiformes* order.

Most great blue observers couldn't care less. Both birds are beautiful and both the crane and the heron wade in shallow water. So similar are the two that "crane" is one of the folk names of the great blue. We will let the scientists argue about how very different they are from each other. Whatever the case, marsh birds and wading birds are very much in the minority since about four-fifths of our feathered friends are land birds.

Feathers are what set them all apart from the other orders of animals, not simply the fact that they fly - for there are mammals

MEET THE GREAT BLUE

that "fly" and birds that do not. The earliest known bird, the *archaeopteryx*, had feathers and wing claws not unlike a bat.

Feathers are quite wonderful evolutionary things. For the great blue heron, their mass far exceeds the quantity of flesh beneath them. Feathers are extremely light but structurally very strong. Their specific individual design is aerodynamic, winglike. While some great blue plumage is fringe and down, most consists of long, supple feathers, each webbed with tiny barbs. If a feather is damaged, it can be repaired by the re-weaving of these barbs through preening, and a molting reveals that if a feather is lost, it will be regenerated.

The number of feathers on a great blue heron is somewhere between the 940 of the rubythroated hummingbird and the 25,000

ABOVE — *Note the singular, small webbing between the first and second toes; even a little bit helps to support the bird on a mushy marsh bottom.* Photo by Robert W. Baldwin

MEET THE GREAT BLUE

of the whistling swan. When the bird molts it is a set process, not just a dropping away of this feather or that one. They are lost in pairs, one from the left and another from the right side. The key element is that the heron is never left in a flightless state, important in the bird's ability to remain mobile for food gathering, migration and escape from danger. Science is still discovering how feathers function in flight and contribute their minute, specific actions as the bird flies through the air.

Flight is, of course, nature's way of feeding and breeding a large percentage of those 9000 species. If all birds were to stay permanently in their winter grounds or feeding places, we would soon have far fewer species and certainly lower bird populations as the land and water could not sustain them. The heron became colonial for this reason, as well as for mating and defense. Incidentally, when a colony of herons migrates en masse, it is called a "siege" of herons, just as we have a flight of doves, a bevy of quail, a skein of geese, a nye of pheasants or an exaltation of larks.

While the feathers enable flight, the possibility of flight is also due in large part to the hollow bones and distribution of lungs and air sacs in the bird's physique. The hollow bones not only hold air but their composition also lessens the weight of the flying creature. The great blue is the norm in the bird world, whereas the loon with its solid bones is not. The lungs and sacs become like little balloons as birds fly and help sustain buoyancy in the air as well as upon water for most waterbirds. Since birds do not perspire, these sacs also serve as regulators of body temperatures

THE IMPORTANCE OF AERODYNAMIC STRUCTURE

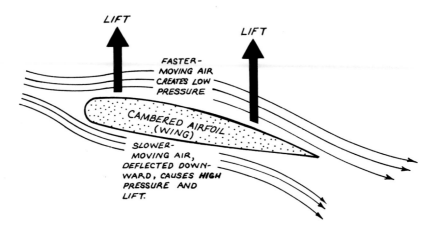

FIGURE 1 — *This diagram shows a cross-section of a typical airplane wing. Its shape is referred to as an "airfoil." This is similar to the shape of not only a bird's wing, but also to each feather that comprises the wing.*

General theory of flight is based on two prominent supportive theories. The first is Sir Isaac Newton's observation that "for every action, there is an equal and opposite reaction." The other is Swiss mathematician Daniel Beroulli's discovery that if the velocity of a fluid (in this case, air) is increased at a particular point, the fluid's pressure is decreased at that same point. To explain why the aerodynamic shape above enables flight to take place, we apply these two theories.

A wing shape with a curved top and relatively flat bottom forces the air moving across the top, curved surface to move faster than the air moving across the bottom surface, since it has more area to cover in the same amount of time as the wing passes through the air.

Applying Bernoulli's law, this would mean that air pressure on the top of the wing a decreased. According the Newton, then, pressure beneath the wing is increased by an equal amount. Couple these with a slight angle to the wing (angle of attack) that deflects oncoming air downward on the underside of the wing that (again, according to Newton's law) causes upward thrust on top of the wings, and lift is produced. So, the faster the wind moves through the air and the greater pressure and deflection are produced, the more lift is developed. This is what enables objects heavier than air to fly.

MEET THE GREAT BLUE

by regulating the utilization of the breathing process.

The *ardea herodias* does live up to its name as being the heron of herons. Ardea in latin means heron, while in Greek *erodios* is the word for heron. The males are virtually indistinguishable from the females, save for being slightly larger.

When we see the great blue either in flight or wading, it is immediately obvious that we are watching a magnificent, beautiful creature. The body plumage tends to be loosely feathered in long strands, especially on the breast and back. The crest is generally a permanent fixture, but during the mating season its development intensifies and, fascinatingly, a pair of quite noticeable plumes, long and slender as filaments, emerge.

The bird's brow and crown are white, but we see that the feathers leading from the eye back to the crest are black. Its neck will be a light grey, made up of mainly short fine feathers at the top but gradually streaks of white, black and rust created by longer ones will end the breast in a great cluster of long plumes. It is the color found on the back and scapulars or shoulder feathers that give the great blue its name, for there we find feathers that are blue-grey. The long tail is what might be considered slate-grey with black-tipped feathers. The undertail coverts are white.

The legs we see trailing behind in flight or moving, camel-like, through the shallows, tend toward grey. That "knee" that seems to be bending backwards, however, is really the bird's heel. The real knee is further up the leg and hidden under feathers. The function of the heel-that-looks-like-a-knee is part of the wading birds' poetry in motion. Over the eons, the body came to depend entirely upon

MEET THE GREAT BLUE

balance in uncertain waters, so the heel of the foot moved upwards to elevate the center of the bird's balance. It also gives the heron that extra spring in its step when leaping into flight at the first sign of danger. A human resemblance might be considered as our foot's arch that extends between our toes and our heel. As the sprinter springs from the blocks to race down the track, it begins with the toes first and then a heel thrust, not unlike the escaping great blue.

The rest of the "leg" is really an extension of the foot that leads to the curiously constructed, webbed toes. They are arranged in a three-forward-one-rear configuration. This allows for better balance under water, and the webbing keeps the lightweight bird from sinking into the sand or mud or the soft sod of a marsh. The heron's toes are particularly interesting in two ways. First, there is not as much webbing as one might imagine, really only between the first and second toe. Second, the heron carries its own feather comb with it at all times, a small hook that is part of its middle toe's talon. It is the only heron to have this preening or cleaning feature.

While we are observing the physical nature of the bird, let's look at them right in the eye—a marvelous mechanism of the great blue. Obviously, a bird's eyes are vital to survival. The eye protects the animal from predators and locates food. The great blue's golden eyes are among its most distinctive traits. Like the loon with its remarkable red eye, the great blue must also be able to see under water in order to see what to catch for dinner. The physiology of birds' eyes is wonderful. By refocusing almost instantly, the heron's eyes can act as telescopes in one instant and then a magnifying glass in another.

PRECEDING SPREAD — *Few birds - only the eagle, the condor and the albatross - exceed the great blue when it comes to wingspan.* Photo by Stephen Kirkpatrick

MEET THE GREAT BLUE

The great blue is what is called "monocular," meaning that each eye has to focus independently of the other. There is a certain binocularity as the heron looks down its beak straight ahead, but its defense against surprise or attack is based upon the placement of the eyes closer to the back of the head than the tip of the beak. Without much movement, the great blue has the ability of 360 degree vision.

Ardea herodias stands at least four feet tall from its feet planted in the marsh mud to the end of its beak. The great blue's wingspan is often more than six feet from tip to tip, as wide as an eagle's. Yet for all this length and breadth, the bird generally weighs only somewhere between five and eight pounds.

ABOVE — *The magnificent mechanism of the eye of the great blue heron allows it to function as a telescope one instant, a magnifying glass the next - fast focus reflex, if you will. It also allows for underwater vision.* Photo by Scott Nielsen

MEET THE GREAT BLUE

Since the Jurassic Age, 135 million years ago, the earth has possessed birdlike animals. This is not far from the time that paleontologists believe the evolutionary "branching" took place that created the creatures of the land, the sea, and the air. The scaly feet of birds is one of the residuals of that time of environmental selection, back to their reptilian incarnation.

Considering that heron-like birds have been wading the shallow waters of the world for somewhere between 40-70 million years, we might appreciate these wonderful birds as an extraordinary success story. We must remember, though, the fairly recent threat to their survival by plume hunters and the potential threat of pollution or destruction of habitats today.

ABOVE — *The green-backed heron is a short-form member of the heron family. Photo by Kim Harris*

Relatives And Friends

Great blue herons do not have the amazingly large family that one finds with some species, such as the finch with its 436 species. In our part of the world, there are a dozen great blue heron relatives and one or two subspecies. There are four distinct heron groups: bitterns, tiger herons, night herons, and day herons. Here is the American family:

- The black-crowned night heron
- The yellow-crowned night heron
- The universal bittern
- The American bittern
- The least bittern
- The green-backed heron
- The great white heron
- The great American white egret
- The reddish egret
- The blue heron
- The Louisiana heron
- The California heron
- The Ward's heron
- The snowy heron
- The eastern great blue heron
- The great blue heron

Contemporary bird guides, such as Roger Tory Peterson's *Field Guide to the Birds: Eastern Land and Water Birds* or *Birds of North America* by Robbins, Bruun, and Zim have their own ways of dealing with species and subspecies. Peterson perhaps expresses it best with, "Subspecies have a meaning to the student of bird distribution and evolution, and are of practical value to conservation and wildlife management practices, but they should not concern the field amateur."

FOLLOWING SPREAD — *Wildlife preserves provide shared habitat for double-crested cormorants and great blues.* Photo by Robert W. Baldwin

RELATIVES AND FRIENDS

Translated, that means that Ward's Heron, the California and eastern great blues are regional variations that should not be thought of as totally exclusive. Except that Peterson adds a very interesting dimension to these subspecies when he notes that while they are "fundamentally the same bird and capable of interbreeding...they will not under ordinary circumstances hybridize."

When it comes to classifications, though, it is interesting to note that the first great blue was officially logged into ornithological records in 1758 on the shores of Hudson Bay. Audubon himself sighted the white heron one hundred years later on the Florida Keys, and another birder, named Ward, found a subspecies in 1882 in another part of Florida. In 1901, an observer named Chapman discovered a variation among the Queen Charlotte Islands, and two years later someone saw a great blue on Indefatigable Island of the Galapogos and recognized it as a subspecies.

The global distribution of the heron family is almost total and contains about 60 species altogether, including the short necked, short legged, black-crowned night heron, so popular in Japan that centuries ago the shogun elevated it to the status of aristocracy and considered it a messenger carrying communications from the divinity. Yet herons are not one of the central threads in the cultural fabric of most peoples. In European literature of tales and legends, there are numerous stories about swans and certainly storks and the characters of Mother Goose and Henny Penny. There are stories of green canaries, nightingales, crows and sparrows, parrots and golden cockerels and the golden goose. There are even sets of tales about "troll birds" in Scandinavia. In

RELATIVES AND FRIENDS

fact, the Grimm brothers and Hans Christian Andersen found many sources for tales about most popular birds, save the heron who does not find that particular latitude hospitable.

Still, the stork's and swan's domination of Europe's folk tales is puzzling. While the stork will roost traditionally on urban chimney stacks in most of Europe's seacoastal cities, and while the swan's mystery has become cultivated on carefully controlled ponds and riverbanks throughout the Continent—the heron seems to have selected a different course of migration and habitation. The grey heron is, ironically, one of Europe's most protected birds yet does not significantly play a role in its folklore.

ABOVE — *The down-curved beak distinguishes the white ibis.*
Photo by Kim Harris

RELATIVES AND FRIENDS

From North America, the migratory or residential patterns of the great blue heron can extend as far west as the Galapagos Islands and as far north as Greenland. Going much farther west, about 5,000 miles, we find the migratory straits of Pacifica, which include Australia and New Zealand. The heron family is also a significant part of African ornithology, both along the Mediterranean and Red Seas as well as the countryside south of the Sahara Desert

What is important to consider, however, is the fact that the great blue heron is exclusively a creature of the Western Hemisphere, just as the grey heron is singularly European and the Goliath heron belongs to Africa. The great blue of the Galapagos Islands off South America's coast is really the same as the one seen on Blue Lake in Wisconsin, save for the fact that the Galapagos great blue heron never leaves Indefatigable Island as it is a permanent resident sharing its habitat with the world's most exotic creatures. It is completely without fear of strangers.

The feathered friends of the great blue are not legion, since wading birds tend to work the same feeding and roosting spaces at prescribed, safe distances. However, one can find cormorants in the same rookeries as the great blue heron and its relatives, and ducks will feed along the same shallows as the long-legged bird. All the while, there is a grudging respect for each other's territories. Spoonbills, ibises, flamingos—all of which tend to maintain very large colonies—will occupy the same winter feeding grounds as the herons.

OPPOSITE — *The snowy egret, whose glorious plumage nearly led to its extinction. Photo by Kim Harris*

Seasons of Flyways and Byways

Without the migratory instinct, the great blue would languish and probably starve slowly in its winter habitat. It would also degrade or inhibit the entire mating process, which only takes place after the siege migrates. The winter feeding has had two basic purposes: to strengthen the red muscles needed to fly to the nesting ground and to prepare for the annual ritual of breeding and hatching.

When we consider the North American distribution of the great blue heron, little explanation is needed for its tremendous popularity—ranking alongside that of the loon. The great blue roughly squares its habitat between Hudson Bay and an iota of southern Alaska with the edges of South America and the Galapagos Islands offshore of Ecuador.

People living near the bayous and marshes of the American South have the chance to see members of the heron family year round, since a number of the smaller species never leave the warm waters. Generally, the solitary, non-flocking great white heron stays in southern Florida and the Keys, and there are those ornithologists who believe that the *ardea occidentalis* is so closely related to the great blue as to be merely one that has retained its "white phase." This heron, however is not to be confused with

---

OPPOSITE — *Surrounded by the drying evidence of a shrinking pool, and finding less and less food within, a great blue begins to sense the need to seek new sources of nourishment. Some researchers believe that these types of seasonal cues trigger the migration instinct.* Photo by Dusty Perin

another large, white wading bird we normally see along the edges of northern waterways.

The common egret (*casmerodius albus*) lacks the crest and the long breast feathers of the two great herons. In flight, the common egret also curves its neck into an even more radical S-shape than the herons. There are also snowy egrets and cattle egrets. The latter bird is one of the those ornithological rarities: a non-native bird that has thrived and multiplied. The cattle egret came to our part of the world from Africa less than a half-century or so ago. No one knows how it travelled the distance, but there are suppositions such as cattle boats, zoo escapes, and even lost pets.

The first one was seen in the South American country of Guyana just as World War Two was about to begin. Nobody paid much attention because of its similarity in size and whiteness to the snowy egret. However, by the end of the Korean War, it was known to be breeding in western Canada. At the time of John Kennedy's death, Florida bird counters could estimate that there were 30,000 in that state alone. Now, in the 1990s, the *bubulcus ibis* roams most the South, standing on the backs of herds of cattle, feeding on insects and mites just as its African brothers and sisters do, and there is some northern migration from the Great Lakes to the St. Lawrence River.

Only two other herons, the small green-backed heron (*butorides virescens*) and the black-crowned night heron (*nycticorax nyticorax*), come close to roaming as widely as the great blue. Their shapes, coloring and sizes, however, make them easily distinguishable from the grandest member of the family.

OPPOSITE — *Many in the heron family share the same migratory routes. There is a theory that this great white heron is merely a different color phase of the great blue... all dressed up in a clean, white suit, so to speak. Photo by Lynn M. Stone*

SEASONS OF FLYWAYS AND BYWAYS

Still, there are waterways in which the competition for summer feeding and even nesting will include, at some times, four or five angular, relatively tall wading birds, including the great blue.

We might compare the great blue's migratory distribution with one of its cousins, the reddish egret, *dichromanassa rufescens*. Its migration is almost nonexistent, and its general feeding grounds are limited to Baja California, the Florida Keys, and a couple of tiny coastal areas of southeast Texas and the Acapulco area of Mexico. Its range is a few hundred square miles, compared to the tens of thousands of square miles belonging to the flyway of the great blue.

The great blue certainly has the equipment for effortless flight. Its feathers and bone structure, with minimal bodyweight, its six-foot wingspan and lanky four-foot frame physically create a perfect, long-distance flying machine. If indeed, the true mission in a bird's life is to fly, the great blue heron ranks among the Andean condors and the seaspanning albatross.

The range and the power of flight of the great blue heron are the reasons this beautiful bird is part of most of our lives, at one time or another. So prevalent is the presence of this bird and the impression it makes on all who see it, that it has shown up in a range of literature, both classic and popular. "I can tell you are an intelligent man, Johnnie. One difference between your country and mine," said the man from Honduras in Barry Gifford's *Wild at Heart*. They are talking about Johnnie's heritage from the Cayman Islands where "it does not pay to reveal one's intelligence. I am reminded of the time I saw a blue heron walking next to a river.

PRECEDING SPREAD — *The little blue heron often migrates with its larger cousin. This richly pigmented specimen, hidden by its habitat, scouts out dinner.* Photo by Stephen Kirkpatrick

OPPOSITE — *The tri-colored night heron, bluer than its more common cousin, is not found in the Atlantic and Gulf states of America.* Photo by Kim Harris

SEASONS OF FLYWAYS AND BYWAYS

He looked like a Chinese gentleman in a blue coat wobbling along the rocks. He appeared extremely vulnerable and defenseless, yet he was undoubtedly a survivor." This passage also reveals the innate respect that the great blue demands from its observers.

Howard Mead, owner and editor in chief of **Wisconsin Trails** magazine writes, "In all our years of canoeing the rivers of Wisconsin, we have found the great blue heron to be the river equivalent of the loon to the northern lakes, a constant companion." In fact, he recalled that the first picture his wife took and published in their magazine was that of a great blue standing regally on the riverbank.

From the floodplains of the Mississippi to its great delta to the

ABOVE — *Although seeming a distant and far-removed possibility, the least bittern is a relative of the great blue heron.*
Photo by Stephen Kirkpatrick

SEASONS OF FLYWAYS AND BYWAYS

northern tributaries that feed the great river eventually, the great blue is everywhere. When one looks at the flyway and lifecycle pattern of this heron, we see what might appear graphically as a giant oak tree. The great root structure in the South that provides winter feeding—and some year-round residence—with the trunk being the Mississippi Valley and the flatlands of the Great Plains. The spreading limbs and leaves of the upper migratory image are spread between Nova Scotia and Alaska.

The great distances and span of great blue migration are due in large part to the existence of the bird's prevalent "red flight muscles." Wingspread means everything to the hovering condor or eagle or hawk because it enables riding the updrafts. For the heron, the wingspread provides distance, because the flow of its blood to the muscles is intricately woven with the ability to convert food into energy. This also goes back to the numerous air sacs that help cool the metabolic rate of conversion of food to energy, thereby allowing the great blue to eat and fly with equanimity.

We should not confuse the great blue or any other migratory bird with the Wright brothers' invention or the attempts of Icarus and his father to fly. Migration is no pleasure cruise. It is a "flight for life," if you will. It is the instinctual behavior that allows the great blue, like all other long distance ranging birds, the ability to sustain basic life — to consume food and mate, nest and raise their young in environments which can support all these activities.

Migration has been part and parcel of the life cycle of the great blue since the beginning of at least its documented history. The word *migration* itself derives from the Latin *migrare* or "to go from

SEASONS OF FLYWAYS AND BYWAYS

one place to another." And such ancient texts as the book of Jeremiah of the Old Testament in the Bible states, "Yea, the stork in heaven knoweth her appointed times; and the turtle and the heron and the swallow observe the time of their coming..."

So, for the great blue, for 50 million years, the impulse has been to leave with the angle of the sun. There is that eternal question: Does it begin with its setting at a certain angle when the marshes and river borders begin to crust with ice or when the ice melts? Which comes first, the multiplication of food or its diminution? The frogs, turtles, minnows and other food sources begin to multiply with the coming of the sun or retreat before the invasion of the cold and snow, as they have their own programmed processes to follow.

Like one-third of the 9,000 species of birds, the heron must move on with the changing of the sun's path and the coming of the cold. Unlike the bear or the chipmunk who binge-eat so they can retreat to a place warmed by their own bodies, where they enter a sleep humans only dream about, herons, as well as other birds, know that when certain geometric, geographical, and physiological matrices converge they must fly.

Many believe the heron's migration is due to "photoperiodism." This relates to the loss of seasonal light, and it is thought to generate endocrine activity in the family, causing them to migrate south. Yet consider the migration we all watch with anticipation: the clouds of blackbirds, the great formations of geese and ducks, the strings of fowl that follow directions scientists today are still trying to understand. There is tremendous depletion of energy on

OPPOSITE — *Another fellow flyer along the great blue's migration routes, the yellow-crowned heron nevertheless has its own agenda.* Photo by Kim Harris

SEASONS OF FLYWAYS AND BYWAYS

migrations, an incredible puzzle of navigation, and the consummate battle with weather. There are more questions than answers.

There are a number of phenomena that science has not yet been able to comprehend. Migration is one. Does the great blue navigate by stars and our own sun? Are routes taught and programmed by the parents of the young, so that the bird always knows "Turn right by the big pond as the sun sets and fly until you see the crooked bend in the river and then stay the night in the marsh with the six dead trees?"

That was the way that our earliest pilots charted their courses. Reading the memoirs of Charles Lindbergh provides insights into the navigation techniques of our species' first "birds." But no one really understands how the great bird migrations continue regardless of climatological obstacles and geographic alterations. In fact, there are many things that we are sure we do not know. Does the great blue read magnetic north genetically? Is ultraviolet light a factor in reading landscapes? Do birds create a kind of low-intensity sonar, as whales and dolphins do, to determine configurations of land below? Does a bird's eye analyze the polarity of light differently? Are there internal, mini-barometers inside the birds that react to climatic and geographic changes? Are there odors that emanate from a flight path that only the birds recognize? Then there are questions of humidity alterations, temperature variations. It has also been suggested that birds might have the ability to analyze atmospheric electric fields. Those of us who read the skies in migration times, spring and fall, rarely glimpse or note the singular bird on the wing. Most birds are group-oriented, at least as far as migration is concerned, spring or fall.

SEASONS OF FLYWAYS AND BYWAYS

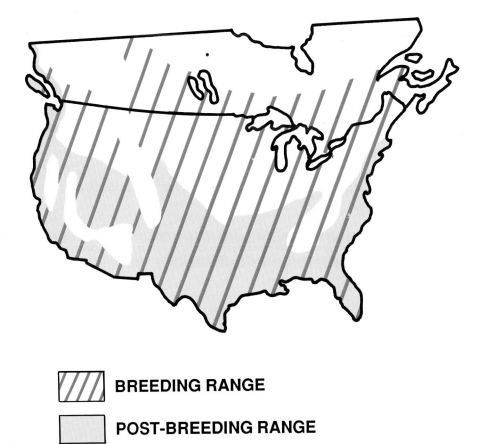

///// BREEDING RANGE

POST-BREEDING RANGE

FIGURE 2 — *The Great Blue Heron throughout an area extending from southern parts of Canada in the north to Mexico, southern Florida and Cuba (except in the high mountains) in the south. After breeding, they disperse to the north in Alaska, central Canada, and non-breeding areas of the United States. They winter from coastal British Columbia through the central U.S. and southern New England all the way south to the upper regions of South America.*

Feeding Time

Whenever we consider the part that food-gathering plays in the life of the great blue, it is imperative to begin with the bird's great beak. It is a formidable tool and a weapon. A wildlife biologist working in Canada provides the account of a couple of bird-banders, people who were spending a research summer in contact with birds in their various habitats. The size of the great blue heron required one person to hold the upper body while the other struggled to attach the identification band.

A four-foot bird, with a neck of about 18", to which is attached a very strong pointed spear, is not to be treated casually. The result was that the scientist holding the wildly flailing neck and beak did not hold on tight enough and the bird actually pierced his skull, resulting in the instantaneous and tragic death of the researcher. James Audubon almost lost his favorite dog because of his ignorance of the potential danger of the great blue heron's great weapon.

"I landed on Indian Bay," he wrote, "and went shopping for white herons" (Florida's version of the great blue) with his Newfoundland, Plato, "a well-trained and most sagacious animal." When Audubon located the heron, he ordered the dog to go near them, but not to hunt or hurt them. America's greatest outdoorsman recalled, "They waited until he went within striking distance, when the largest suddenly struck him with its bill and hung to his nose...birds of this species commonly aim at the eye."

OPPOSITE — *Being obvious, because it is quietly so, has never been a disadvantage to the great blue heron as a hunter.* Photo by Bill Marchel

FEEDING TIME

One does not go lightly into combat with a heron.

It is equally as important to the life of the great blue because it is its long beak, which is considerably longer than the rest of its head, that feeds itself and its young. The wings of the bird are arms without hands, so the great blue's beak serves that multi-purpose function. Not only does it spear and gather food, it is a vicious weapon, a talented builder of nests, and along with the foot's unique hook, the beak is crucial for good grooming. Beaks are not the bird's nose, for few birds actually act on odors. They are more like a horn made of a hard epidermis that opens and closes, functioning like our thumb and forefinger to pinch something to pick it up. The main function, though, of the great

ABOVE — *Although it may appear that this great blue is burying its head in the water much as an ostrich might bury its head in the sand, this is far from the case. For while the ostrich attempts to hide itself underground, the heron's head underwater becomes a lethal spear, striking like lightning at its prey.* Photo by Scott Nielsen

ABOVE — *The great blue locates and captures its prey.* Photo by Scott Nielsen

FEEDING TIME

blue's beak, like those of the loon or the kingfisher or the oystercatcher and tern is to catch food.

When it comes to food, most herons could probably be considered primarily fish-catchers. However, they are truly omnivorous carnivores, eating almost anything that will fit in their gullets. One of the few threats to herons is the problem of occasionally trying to swallow something too large and choking to death. When it is "grazing" the shorelines, the great blue is hunting, especially during the time it is half-responsible for feeding the young back in the nest, for just about anything that moves: fish, frogs, small turtles, snakes. Unlike some waders, the great blue apparently does not like living food, so if the first thrust of the spearlike beak doesn't kill the fish, the amphibian or the reptile, the heron will "play" with it until it does die, or the great blue will find something to spear it on — a log, a rock, the shore. The bird has learned over time to swallow everything headfirst. It even knows to avoid some species like the catfish, which have sharp spines that might cause problems, such as when the great blue is stocking up on food for the nestlings, and the dinner must be regurgitated later. After swallowing the food, herons are quite often seen cleaning their beaks in the water before continuing the quest for more.

Great blue herons also feed in meadows and marshes. They will pursue field mice, shrews, slow pocket gophers or ground squirrels, small muskrats, toads and frogs, lizards, crawfish, crabs, coastal shrimp, grasshoppers, and dragonflies. They even rob the nests of lowland birds, such as blackbirds. A familiar sight, therefore, can be a great blue pursued by a flock of redwinged black birds. More than likely, the giant bird has had its way with hatchlings before being chased off.

FEEDING TIME

At least one birdwatcher has seen a great blue flying away with a half-dozen blackbirds perched on its back, pecking away. Another observed a heron being pursued by a flock that just wouldn't go away, upon which the great blue did a loop-the-loop and whitewashed the blackbirds with a cloud of guano, after which the birds left it alone.

The great blue is a boon to nature's culling process, for the fish that it takes from lakes and streams are not usually gamefish fingerlings. Most likely they are the species that most fishermen would gladly see removed. Izaak Walton, one of the first fishing writers, once wrote in *The Complete Angler* that one could reliably depend upon good fishing downstream of a heron.

However, as any fishery worker will confirm, they do prove to be a blight upon the cultivation of game fish stocks in fisheries and hatcheries, or ponds where frogs are raised for food. Only then are the rules that protect the great blue heron with the Federal Migratory Bird Treaty negotiated to be waived.

The great blue feeds day and night, although the favorite time is just before dawn and dusk. It has been known to use its wings as shade to see prey better, as well as to flap them and create movement beneath their feet. They can feed in the surf of Florida's and the Gulf Coast seas. Observers have seen them drop out of a migrating flock to spear into a shoal of fish along a shore. It is not unheard of to have great blues spotted in swimming pools, artificially created ponds of the suburbs and golf courses, or a backyard after a flood. Not unlike the seagulls of the mall parking lots, the great blue will go where the food is, including drenched meadows and sloughs or canals during run-off times.

OPPOSITE — *Then the great blue arches its long neck for the coup de grace.* Photo by Scott Nielsen

FEEDING TIME

As with mating, the great blue has over the eons developed feeding actions that have been given such names as *peering over, standing, wading, facing down, walking slowly, wing flicking, foot stirring, jumping feet first, hopping, hovering, standing flycatching, pecking* and *wingflicking.* As most of us observers could rightly guess, 90% of a great blue's foraging is spent in the *standing* or *walking slowly* modes. Thus, it takes little imagination to conceive of this angular bird moving along a shoreline or just staying immobile, awaiting dinner to come to its table.

It is the remaining ten percent, however, that give glamour to the great blue's fishing techniques. None, however, is more exotic than the black heron's *canopy feeding.* While this heron is less than half the size of the great blue and its range is subequatorial Africa, the intricacy of its cunning hunting is unparalleled in ornithology. The black heron actually creates a wraparound umbrella of its wings and body feathers, under which it is totally shaded from the sun's path along the equator, thereby providing the bird with the ability of seeing its quarry under a canopy of perfect shade and protecting in its black-feathered heat absorption at beak-level the capacity of spiking its prey.

Wingflicking and *Foot Stirring* are two feeding techniques that depend on a certain capability for reasoning apparently possessed by the great blue heron. While standing in slow-moving or still water, the heron occasionally finds a lack of movement by its intended prey, the small fish that inhabit these waters. Without such movement, the light reflections that usually catch the eye of the heron do not occur, making it difficult for the bird to spot its targets.

FEEDING TIME

On these occasions, the heron will sometimes resort to *wingflicking*, which is when it dips the tip of its wing into the water and flicks it rapidly, causing the fish to scatter, thereby making themselves more visible to the heron. Another similar technique is foot stirring, during which the bird swirls its foot about in the water (usually after being alerted to the presence of something brushing past its leg) with much the same effect.

One expert has observed more than 30 different feeding movements of herons. Each one has its purpose, just as a good bass or trout fisherman will know his or her lures and bait, flies and lines when it comes to foraging a particular path of water. While we can easily visualize the *standing* and *walking slowly*

ABOVE — *Food might be a frog, crayfish, even a snake.* *Photo by Scott Nielsen*

FEEDING TIME

ABOVE — *The last step is a neat "flip and twist", which makes sure the great blue's dinner goes down the gullet headfirst, thus avoiding the possibility of injury from bones, sharp, spiny fins, and other possible complications.* Photo by Scott Nielsen

FEEDING TIME

methods, it is the *hovering, plunging, jumping feet first, swimming/feeding, wingflicks, hopping* and the *diving* that add to the arsenal of the great blue's hunting legend.

To *hover* is to become a four-foot-long, six-foot-winged hummingbird, essentially, for that is what the great blue does. We might think twice of the bird's relatively slow wing movement in flight, which is about two or three beats per second. Consider that in the circle flight of nuptial bliss the wing beats are decreased, apparently to create a specific sound of feathers on the wind. If this incredible bird is able to regulate its wingspeed at short notice, then it is not difficult to picture the lightweight but greatly-spanned bird achieving a hovering dimension that enables it to stab at the fish or food observed below.

We've all seen movie footage showing how pelicans fly to a certain altitude, point earthward, fold their wings and dive. The kingfisher does the same thing. So does the great blue heron, believe it or not. Not only does it make that graceful head-first *dive* into water, without that last minute militant folding of wings. It can also jump out of the sky, feet-first, right into the water after its prey-the *jumping feet first* tactic. It seems that the great blue will do whatever it takes to find food.

The *swimming/feeding* method is almost a "dead duck" gimmick. The great blue, although not immune to feather-drenching and drowning, can swim on the surface due to its great wingspread and its minimal bodyweight. We must realize that the great blue is neither a Canada goose nor a swan, much less a duck. What the great blue does is spread its wings, cupping air underneath, head poked under the water; it floats on the water's

---

PRECEDING PAGE — *The impeccable personal hygiene regimen of the great blue heron might lead an observer to believe that the bird's vanity exceeds a simple regard for cleanliness.* Photo by Scott Nielsen

FEEDING TIME

surface and trolls with the current or the wind. Instinctively, the bird knows that its oiled feathers will repel water for only a short time and the air trapped between the water and the wings and the individual feathers on the body will not last long. Therefore this technique is used only for moments, possibly before flying off for loafing at noon or dusk, for drying out and preening off the surface water flotsam and jetsam.

Along the upper Mississippi River's floodplain, David Thompson monitored with an airplane and a team of ground observers the flight and feeding behavior of the great blues rookery on the Bad Axe River.

The scene is late May on the Upper Mississippi River National

ABOVE — *A million or more years have imprinted upon the great blue's psyche the felt need to be as clean as possible, and upon its physiology the agility to achieve that goal.* Photo by Scott Nielsen

FEEDING TIME

Wildlife and Fish Refuge, south of La Crosse, Wisconsin. The mating season is over, the pairs have settled into their nests, the clutch of eggs has been laid, and the parents are alternating the incubation times. The sun is beginning to rise above the bluffs that overshadow the heronry, and the great blue designated as first feeder issues a *quuuaarrk* and flaps its great wings, lifting quickly off the seemingly teetering nest and into the air.

Travelling at about 25 miles per hour, wings slowly wagging at about once every three or four seconds, the great blue heron flies south over Spring Coulee, past an egret rookery on Coon Creek, and upstream from the Genoa National Fish Hatchery, where the rangers warily guard their ponds from interloping great blues. At the Bad Axe River, the bird angles east-northeast, upstream.

Depending upon the great blue's past experience, the journey may be only three miles or as far away as a dozen before the site is spied and the descent is made. For the next two and one-half hours, our great blue heron will graze the shoreline of the river or wander off into the treeline along the shore. They are still wearing their pre-molting cryptic plumage and the pockets of shade and shadows will protect them from predators that never seem to come—so successful is the protective coloring or their innate paranoia.

The great blue is an efficient fisher, but also a tidy one. It will even leave the water as the need to defecate arises, rather than cloud the river's flow. While the bird seems to prefer quiet pools and eddies, it does not avoid the turgid flowages where its breakfast is more difficult to see. Some birders reckon that the

OPPOSITE — *Loafing time – those hours between feeding periods and nesting or mating – is spent tidying up while digesting meals.*
Photo by Scott Nielsen

FEEDING TIME

great blue feels the fish swimming around its legs when they cannot be seen, and spears them as a fisherman pulls on the rod when the hook seems faintly tugged.

The great blue will browse against the current, moving upstream, working the way toward fish that are facing the path of food coming toward them and are less aware of the predator approaching their tails. The bird will spear its prey, and perform various killing styles before ingesting the creature head-downward.

After generously feeding, when the great blue might actually eat its own weight in fish, frogs, snakes, turtles, and so on, it is R & R time. In ornithological terms, "loafing" is comprised of those hours when the bird cleans and preens itself and dozes in the noonday sun. The great blue is no stranger to loafing.

It will leave its feeding zone and find a perch, whether on a tree limb, a treetop or even a muskrat lodge. There the great blue performs a fascinating ritual. When we usually see the bird, it is in the fishing mode, statuesque, charismatic, solitary. Yet it is the hours after feeding that present the most fascinating portrait of what might seem to be a vainglorious bird, who might find its equivalent in the cat family after a sumptuous supper.

The great blue must rank among the highest of hyper-hygienic creatures, for its "loafing" is really a cleansing process that covers the entire four-foot body and six-foot wingspan. Like many waterfowl or wading birds, the great blue heron has a waterproofing system. For the great blue it is a gland found at the base of its tail. The gland secretes an oil that the bird withdraws and then paints its feathers with the substance, thereby

OPPOSITE — *Reaching back like a contortionist, the great blue preens its back plumes, applying an oil secreted by a gland beneath its tail feathers, to ensure water repellence.* Photo by Scott Nielsen

FEEDING TIME

replenishing the oily nature of those feathers exposed to being watered down or washed away.

The most fascinating dimension of this loafing time, though, is the utilization of the patches of powderdown feathering. There are typically three patches of this powdery fluff. Other birds have powderdown concentrations, but it is difficult to find evidence that these are put to the same cleansing use as that of the great blue. The easily disintegrated substance of feather dust is spread, using its beak over those areas, especially the legs and lower body, whereupon it absorbs the swamp scum, the fish oil, the variety of slime that is picked up while wandering the shorelines.

By itself, this is an intriguing natural phenomenon, but the great blue's tools of application appear to be unique within the kingdom of birds. The middle talon of its foot has a small comb, a curved, serrated hook used in preening. Most great blue heron birders relegate this physical attribute to merely preening — the combing of feathers. It does appear logical, however, that the comb is exactly what is needed to probe and rake the powderdown patches for the dust that can be used as an absorbent. Only a few wingbeats off the loafing roost and the impregnated granules fly off as the great blue heron returns to the rookery and allows its mate the time to feed and preen. Part of the loafing recess is digestion time when inedible parts will be spit out.

The great blue heads home when this toilet procedure is completed. The act of landing on the nest is one of nature's rare ungraceful moments. This is not ballet on the wing. "It seemed to me that nature made a mistake," wrote Howard Mead, outdoors

---

OPPOSITE — *Grooming is essential to the bird's survival, removing fish oils, marsh muck and other flight-inhibiting residue.* Photo by Scott Nielsen

FEEDING TIME

editor/publisher, "as if evolution took a detour. Why was a bird like this up in the trees instead of on the ground or in the water, where it obviously belongs?"

At the end of its occupation of feeding and preening, the great blue flies north, up the Mississippi toward the heronry. It will make that clumsy landing on the roost seemingly designed by a child playing with sticks and twigs. Upon its arrival, the mate will ascend into its own pattern of flight and head off toward its own feeding zone. The feeding and preening rituals will continue until the sun begins to set and it is time to return home. The pair will share the time that night on the nest.

Everything will change when the clutch hatches.

OPPOSITE — *Tucked away in the great blue's plumage are a number of special, downy patches that serve as absorbent matter to work on oily build-up or mud.* Photo by Scott Nielsen

FOLLOWING PAGE — *The bird's unique middle-talon comb rakes through the downy patch, distributin it to those places in need of sponging. Later, as the bird flies or the wind blows through the feathers, the dust falls away, having done its job.* Photo by Scott Nielsen

FEEDING TIME

ABOVE — *The bird stands like a royal sentinel, its plumage glistening in the light and flowing cleanly in the breeze.* Photo by *Scott Nielsen*

FOLLOWING SPREAD — *Then it's either back to fishing or on to the rookery.* Photo by Scott Nielsen

FEEDING TIME

OPPOSITE — *Plumbing the summer wallows for supper.* Photo by Bill Marchel

ABOVE — *Success!* Photo by Bill Marchel

FEEDING TIME

ABOVE — *Try as one might, it's hard to be inconspicuous when one is a great blue heron.* Photo by Bill Marchel

ABOVE — *If there are fish to be found along the shore, chances are there will also be great blue herons.* Photo by Lynn M. Stone

FEEDING TIME

ABOVE — *So, like many other tourists, great blues stroll Florida's sandy shores in the wintertime. Photo by Stephen Kirkpatrick*

OPPOSITE — *Gracefulness is not always part of fishing. Photo by Bill Marchel*

FEEDING TIME

OPPOSITE — *The occasional dunking does not enhance one's plumage; another reason for loafing time.* Photo by Lynn M. Stone

ABOVE — *The beginning of a canopy feeding pose.* Photo by Dusty Perin

FEEDING TIME

PRECEDING SPREAD — *Among lily pads, in ponds or swamps... the great blue still stalks.* Photo by Dusy Perin

ABOVE — *Cruising for food in the widespread marshes.* Photo by Robert McKenzie

OPPOSITE — *In the backwaters, there is time for solitary, sunset loafing.* Photo by Lynn M. Stone

Family Life And The Rookery

Courtship takes place after the northern migration, when all the great blues are gathered in one of their few multiple, flocking movements. It should be noted that the great blue, as romantic a creature as it is, is not a romancing bird, coupling for life and living forlornly after the loss of a mate, like one of E.B. White's swans.

The great blue is among the most willingly independent birds around. True, they are colonial, but only at certain times of the migratory and mating calendar. In most cases, the heron is not a polygamous bird, mating with more than one female. But in the mating season, there can be occasions of polygamy when a clutch of eggs has been destroyed or hatchlings lost.

For most of the year great blue herons are very solitary, singular birds. There are only three times (at northern migration, during breeding and at southern migration) in their annual lives when they act colonially. This is not unusual, for hunting creatures are generally loners, whether they be eagles, herons, rails, kingfishers or nightjars. When it comes time to travel and subsist, however, cooperation and community are natural to the great blue heron. When it comes to migration it also means first setting in motion the survival of the breed.

Herons have some trouble identifying themselves, probably because they don't allow each other to come too closely, even in mating time. This is understandable when one considers the fact

OPPOSITE — *When a nest is full of great blues, the adults with their long, tuftlike crests are easy to identify.* Photo by Lynn M. Stone

FAMILY LIFE AND THE ROOKERY

that the great blue heron's courtship arena can be as long as a half-mile and as wide as two football fields. It helps to know how extensive the ritual breeding movements are.

Spacing proscribing tolerance and territory are critical to the great blue. Even when clustering for the function of breeding, the tolerable distance is measured in yards. Of course, we can ascribe this to the two yards or more of wingspan that must be unfolded at a moment's notice, or to the distance required for flight, instinctive comprehension of the limitations of habitat and feeding. Plus, one theorist believes that the great blue realizes that the time spent fighting over territory means less time for feeding, which is definitely the *raison d'etre* of herons.

As antisocial the heron might seem to be, its loyalty is constant during the nest-building through the hatchling development. There is no question that, once the young are capable of leaving the nest, the parents immediately begin looking for a better place to feed. Thus, their second phase of migration will usually occur, for within a hatching and fledgling rookery the youngest know only the directions of feeding resources they have observed of the parents.

As with those animal species for which survival and endurance requires the transferral of the strongest seminal swimmers in the genetic pool, the great blues do compete with each other for dominant roles in mating. There is often a duel of beaks, but it seems more symbolic than life-death fighting. The mating dance of the male great blue is not as long as it is with other birds, but there is stretching and the flouncing of wings. As the female returns the compliments, the two become about as courtly as they

FAMILY LIFE AND THE ROOKERY

will ever be, as one will preen the other's pair of long plumes they have grown especially for the occasion. It is actually a kind gesture as the back of the neck is about the only spot that the toe hook does not reach. So it becomes a kind of bonding act, but after copulation, the two will show very little affection or thought for the other's comfort and appearance.

In many ways, theirs is more a matter of tradition and convenience than a "happy marriage." The innate need to couple and procreate, to propagate their species onto the next generation is the strength of their alliance. They will need each other's help in the strengthening of the nest or building it, incubation, the brooding, the feeding and rearing of the young herons. Normally,

ABOVE — *With the onset of the mating season, it is time for teamwork with a singular purpose.* Photo by Lynn M. Stone

THE STRAIGHT-NECKED POSITION OF THE CIRCLE FLIGHT

Figure 3 — *The Circle Flight behavior is, generally, uncommon for either sex. It is occasionally used by unpaired males to move from their nests to an alternate display site, such as a nearby vacant nest. This serves as an approach technique for the satellite females, as they tend to land closer to the courting male each time they perform a circle flight. During the first days of pairbonding, infrequent circle flights are continued by both sexes. On certain mornings, possibly due to especially suitable weather conditions or to a form of display imitation (called "social facilitation"), entire great blue colonies exhibit unusually frequent circle flights.*

It is believed that for the male great blues, the circle flight serves as an advertisement of the bird's sex, species and general physical vigor. Satellite females probably use this information to decide which males to approach.

Typically, this behavior consists of a straight-necked flight of about 15-30 seconds, during which wingbeats are slightly slower and deeper than usual, producing an audible "whomp" with each stroke. The heron flies in a large circle, usually 50-75 yards in diameter (thus the behavior's name), landing back near its origin.

OPPOSITE — *Old nests are often rebuilt or improved, complete with the rituals of coming and going, often including the circle flight behavior.* Photo by Lynn M. Stone

FAMILY LIFE AND THE ROOKERY

they would never get that close to one another, so it is nature arbitrating a temporary truce between usually very shy and standoffish creatures.

"I confess that I myself might have been skeptical...having been accustomed to find in all places the heron to be a solitary bird, cannot be prevailed upon to believe the contrary, had I not seen with my own eyes the vast multitudes of different species breeding together in certain favorable localities." So writes John James Audubon a century and one-half ago, also apparently referring to the common practice of rookeries being occupied by herons, egrets and other wading birds simultaneously.

Every heron has its own dance of seduction. While there are not too many look-a-like flocks, the evolution of the species has created different mating dances for different birds. Mostly involving feather-spreads and bobbing and weaving, one-steps and two-steps, plus some exciting mano-a-mano fights between competing males, the courtship of the female by the male is always one of male dominance.

Lest this be considered some kind of ornithological chauvinism, it should be recognized that all animals—birds and mammals and aquatic kin—do not do a courtship ritual solely out of vanity or to demonstrate strength. The only reason for courtship rituals is the continuation and sustaining endurance of that creature. The strongest male succeeds in mating because of necessity. If the bird's species is going to survive millions of years, the weakest link is no guarantee of perpetuity. In some animals, possibly herons, sperm displacement is part of the breeding

OPPOSITE — *A great, tall tree in California finds its fate tied to a heronry.* Photo by Robert McKenzie

FAMILY LIFE AND THE ROOKERY

process, and the mass of male ingredients thrust into the ovulation track will prove to "outrank" the lesser inputs from the less potent of the flock or the herd or the pod.

The competition for supremacy in the connection with great blue heron females is visually fascinating. There are various film and video representations of the strangely familiar rituals of different birds mating. For the great blue, it is no less dramatic. "Arena behavior" pits one male against another. There are two aspects of courtship and mating rites: "unpaired" and "paired." As the prospecting male seeks the recruiting female, there is considerable gesturing on the part of each bird. But mainly, the work belongs to the male who must demonstrate his supremacy over his rivals.

ABOVE — *Even the exchange of sticks for nestbuilding has its own prescribed pattern.* Photo by Lynn M. Stone

FAMILY LIFE AND THE ROOKERY

The herons, giants of the American family, are often forced to find their seasonal mates on a battleground of a multitude of other, smaller members of the family. Post-migration activities are intense and multiple in late spring.

"Let's fight," one male indicates to another. Typically they strut and fret their bachelor time upon the stage of progeneration. The size of the stage or arena varies, but definition of territory is always the concern of the great blue. Fights are duels, not unlike the classical use of foils to decide that terrible moment of confrontation. For the great blue heron, though, its beak is the weapon which of determines who will mate with a certain female.

Ornithologists have established specific descriptions of this courting ritual. There is the *stretch,* the *snap*, the *wing preen, bill duels*, the *circle flight,* and when all is consummated, the *landing call*, the *twig shake, crest raising* and a myriad of other physical gestures. These social signals demonstrate the million-year, timeworn tradition that has kept the population intact.

As Thompson's research team spent days and months studying the feeding cycles of great blues and egrets, similar serious and extended research was completed in 1976 by Douglas Mock and titled, unromantically, "Pair-Formation Displays of the Great Blue Heron." Just to put this kind of scientific, on-site study into perspective, consider that thousands of still photographs were taken plus 1000 feet or more of movie film recording the social activity that leads to mating among great blue herons.

There is what is called *the solo male stage*, when the unpaired male heron selects a site that normally includes a previously used

FAMILY LIFE AND THE ROOKERY

The Fluffed Neck Behavior

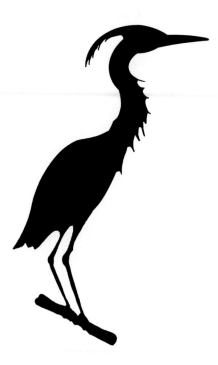

Figure 4 — *As a male heron repeatedly brings sticks to the female during cooperative nest-building, she may greet him with the Fluffed Neck instead of the more common Stretch response. A great blue might also exhibit a fluffed neck as an aggressive response to being swooped at by smaller birds, such as gulls. However, this display is fairly rare in herons' repertoire of behaviors.*

FAMILY LIFE AND THE ROOKERY

nest in a rookery. By the time this "leasing" takes place, the male is at full plumage, as well as with the bright coloring of its legs, and the additional intensity of color added to the lores and the bill. This is the only time when the male great blue looks different from the female great blue.

The bachelor great blues roam their nesting areas, perfectly willing to compete for supremacy and female audiences. To qualify as a bachelor the male has only to fight for the advantage. Interestingly, the female can simply reject male advances and go elsewhere. After all, the male has picked the nesting location and is looking for a co-habitant, a mate. The male great blue is not bashful, showing his prowess to any and all females in the vicinity. This bachelordom is clearly an audition process that will eventually

ABOVE — *A six-pound bird with a seven-foot wingspan carries a slender stick to help build its nest.* Photo by Robert McKenzie

FAMILY LIFE AND THE ROOKERY

lead to the female's ultimate selection of the father of her clutch. When the selection is finally made, the male allows the female to occupy the nest. The ritual is the ultimate dramatic performance. *The stretch* is a key movement, graceful and pointed, almost like a pas de deux, among the most lovely of ballet movements.

For those who have watched this stately stretching, there is a definite choreography to the leg flexes, the bill passes, the abrupt body movements with or without sound, and a documented photographic record of a bending of the body axis beyond 45 degrees, while the legs bend low. Wing extension is also part of the act. This doesn't happen only once. Actually, it is the most common display of bachelor males. It can happen when the female has inserted a single stick into his nest. She can signal him by repetition of his own movements. So basically, *the stretch* is a way of getting to know one another, ("Ain't I handsome, honey?") as well as saying to a male rival, "I'm bigger and better than you, buddy." Meanwhile, female great blues are watching the winners.

Since great blue herons are solitary, yet colonial, birds, there is the need to inform the female that no threat is intended in the approach. At the height of the mating season, which comes soon after arriving in the established, selected heronry or rookery, the birds are also dressed in their most decorative plumage and coloring of legs and bills. *The stretch* is the most conspicuous and lengthy of the great blue's acting repertoire. In the great blue's stretch, we see the bird with all of its feathers at ease, and it will slowly lift its head and swing its bill. Its only sound is that of a low moan that continues through the movement, which continues throughout the entire

---

OPPOSITE — *Perilously perched, testing the limits of the limb, a heron pair performs the copulatory act.* Photo by Robert McKenzie

FAMILY LIFE AND THE ROOKERY

length of the body, from beak tip to talons. Notable is the fact that the crest and scapular plumes stay at rest through this signal.

The bird's bill is arched to its apogee, with its long neck plumes fully extended in the move. The great blue then turns his head slightly to one side, as if to see exactly who is being impressed with his elegance. Also, when the head has reached that point, the bird begins its singularly poignant moan-like call that will continue throughout the raising and lowering of the head. That descent includes a swaying motion of the heron's body, wings often partly extended, as its weight is shifted from one leg to another. It takes much longer to describe the whole stretch than to complete it, as fewer than ten seconds are involved from beginning to end.

There is also a female *stretch*, but this occurs after the mating has commenced. In these cases, the female stretches after receiving the twig the male has brought to help improve the nest, part of the *stick transfer ceremony*. Also during incubation and feeding periods for the clutch, the female and male will signal their willingness to leave the nest in the *nest relief ceremony*. These rituals tend to take less and less time and elaboration as their relationship is established.

The great blue's repertoire of courting gestures rival popular dance steps. For example, there is the *snap*, the *forward*, the *wing preen*, and *crest raising*. The snap involves the plumes of the head, neck, breasts and back. They become erect when the head is moved forward. When the heron's bill and neck are almost completely straight, the bird will bend its legs and clack once with its mandibles, the upper and lower parts of the beak. There are

---

OPPOSITE — *The fabled rookery - a word that derives from the old English ruck, "to squat, as a hen does with its eggs[2]" - this one in California.* Photo by Robert McKenzie

FAMILY LIFE AND THE ROOKERY

high-level and lower-level *snaps*, but the move called the *forward* generally takes the heron closer to the rival or potential mate, whereas the *snap* is usually executed away from the other bird. The snap can also be included in the *stick transfer ritual*, although the clack of the beak is reduced since the bird's mouth has something in it. Although females do the *snap* occasionally, it is usually part of the solo or bachelor stages of the great blue. After pairing and before egg-laying the ritual is no longer used. There are various theories about the "origin" of the *snap*, but the prevalent one attaches significance to its announcement that the bird is a good stick gatherer and a worthy co-builder of nests.

The *wing preen* is another predominantly male gesture, although females have been noted doing it at different times of the pairing process. The movement begins when the heron extends one wing, generally when the bird is next to its possible mate, and then moves its bill along the leading edge of the wing, once or twice, taking only a couple of seconds to complete the demonstration. While it is usually a honing gesture, there are those who may or may not touch the feathers and those who actually nip within the wing during the movement.

Finally, when the pair have chosen to be mates, the *circle flight*, also called the "Nuptial Flight," occurs in the early days of their pairing. What makes this doubly interesting is the fact that it is the only time when the heron flies with its neck extended, like a crane. For as long as a half-minute for males and nearly a minute for females, the birds will circle away and return to the mate, generally once but dual circuits have been observed. In the

OPPOSITE — *It is not unusual for different members of the heron family to share a rookery. The more noise, the better (it serves as a sort of "early warning system "), and everyone learns their own places in colonial heron hierarchy.* Photo by Lynn M. Stone

THE ARCHED NECK BEHAVIOR

Figure 5 — *Other herons in a rookery walking, landing, departing or just flying past may elicit a Neck Arching behavior in great blues. According to Douglas W. Mock's research (The Wilson Bulletin, June 1976), a heron landing within 2 to 10 yards of another will be warned with this gesture. Should the offending bird have the chutzpah to land any closer, violating its "personal space", it risks being physically attacked.*

This behavior has also been observed in response to other stimuli such as: sudden loud noises or the approach of a human to the rookery. When this happens, it is common for many colony members to display the arched neck simultaneously.

OPPOSITE — *For adults, greeting each other is an act of recognition and assurance of safety, rather than an establishment of dominance and submission.* Photo by Lynn M. Stone

FAMILY LIFE AND THE ROOKERY

earliest occasions, the male makes the *circle flights*, with the female repeating it, coming closer and closer to the nest he has selected for their brood. Once the various pairings have been completed in the rookery, it is possible to see on the occasional morning much of the population of the colony making *circle flights*, possibly to finalize the claim on the nest and to formally identify each others' pairbonding.

One of the marvels of the natural world is the variety of behavioral activities that eventually lead to the pairing of males and females. In nearly all cases, the male must demonstrate to the female that he is both capable of defending her and their future brood and also ranks in the hierarchy over other competing

ABOVE — *Some courtship dances are successful; others demand encore performances for different audiences.* Photo by Lynn M. Stone

FAMILY LIFE AND THE ROOKERY

THE UPRIGHT BEHAVIOR

Figure 6 — *Considered to be an attention-getting display, the upright posture seems to be a special signal used mainly in situations where many herons are feeding in areas away from the rookery.*

FAMILY LIFE AND THE ROOKERY

males. In the case of the great blue, which like most herons is very nearly identical in either gender—size is about the only difference—the initiation of the various moves and gestures identifies the males for the females. The more mature males, who have survived numerous migrations and dangers and still are recognized within the males of the colonies as being strongest, are generally the dominant breeders. In fact, the young males in their first two years will not breed, and then in the third year only if there are unpaired females still looking for mates.

There is nothing quite like a great blue heron rookery. Many other birds do build their nests near each other, but none quite like the ungainly heron who does not seem like the nesting type, especially with ten or thirty or a thousand other pairs in the areas trees. However, it should be noted that there are recorded nest-buildings taking place in duckblinds on level ground, like Mark Twain's Moses in the "bullrushes." Scientists have built platforms that nests could be built upon. In rare cases, herons have built isolated, solitary nests on the ground. It should be pointed out, however, that the loss sustained by single nests far exceeds the mortality levels of the rookery conglomeration. Among the grandest have been those built halfway up a 200 foot California redwood.

Wherever there is the equivalent of an apartment building of nests, one encounters three definite, identifiable traits. Since these rookeries are repeatedly used throughout dozens of generations of birds, they are easy to see in flooded forests of a great blue's territory. Over the years they have been so coated with guano as

OPPOSITE — *There is no rule that guarantees a beautiful baby.*
Photo by Lynn M. Stone

FAMILY LIFE AND THE ROOKERY

to almost be luminescently white and leafless. Secondly, the heron might be a bird that does not depend upon scent, but in human terms, especially during fledgling time, an incredible potpourri of odors emanates from a rookery and can be quickly anticipated once one is within nose range. Not only is the guano build-up of decades impressive, there is also the smell of regurgitated dinners that were not found by the young and careless, eager eaters.

Lastly, it is difficult to miss a tall tree that is festooned with nests that can be as wide as four feet and a couple of feet deep, a veritable jumble of sticks and twigs that seem terribly precarious in their construction and balance.

One of the rituals of the newlyweds is that of *stick transfers*. The male will venture into the wilderness and return to the nesting female proudly proffering a twig, a small branch, some pine needles, perhaps some marsh moss or grass, reeds and anything else he thought worthwhile on a flight home from fishing or on the specific nest-building mission. His mate gratefully accepts the gift, and she finds a place to put it, just so. What we really have is a fundamentally stable, solid nest that is composed of a rough exterior that will tolerate most high winds and repel or repulse predators like racoons or eagles, plus having a relatively soft base upon which the coming clutch of eggs will rest and be incubated.

There are those times when the different nesting and identification rituals can produce the unwanted collapse of a nest. It also appears that there is no heron engineering instinct for weight, therefore there are occasions when the weight of the nest

OPPOSITE — *Rookery rituals are many: here is the periodic feeding of the nestlings. Photo by Lynn M. Stone*

STOP-ACTION ILLUSTRATION OF THE FORWARD

Figure 7 — *The Forward display is performed primarily from the nest as a territorial defense. Used by the solo male immediately after choosing a nest site, it is more common in bachelor males and less common in paired males. Females will forward, although less frequently than males, and generally direct this behavior toward satellite females during the mating stage. The Forward involves the heron extending its wings slightly from the sides of its body, retracting its head part way into the shoulders, and erecting all plumes on the head, back and neck. It has been observed among sibling heron hatchlings as early as a few days of age.*

OPPOSITE — *Nothing teaches a nestling to beg but its own empty stomach. The little mouth that makes the most noise becomes the biggest baby bird. Photo by Lynn M. Stone*

FAMILY LIFE AND THE ROOKERY

is so great as to break the limb upon which it has been resting for decades. Indeed, the construction is a complex kind of architecture, beginning with the foundation and leading to the bed of moss and soft materials. While it may not be as intricate as the African hammerhead stork that raises what is actually a roofed house in the confines of tree limbs, the heron's nest is among birddom's largest and most elaborate.

One reason that the mating and nest-building becomes a monogamous situation is the need to achieve it all while the female holds the male's sperm active. It may be that it stays potent for a few minutes or several days, during which the nest must be occupied and improved. After several days, she then lays her clutch.

The clutch of bluish eggs might range from three to seven, and it varies according to the latitude, with the numbers increasing as one goes farther north. The survival rates necessitate this. From the moment of laying, the pair begin a month-long incubation of the eggs. Meanwhile, all around the new parents-to-be are probably dozens of other pairs experiencing the same instinctual experience. Nest tending, egg turning, guarding against predators. It is easy to imagine the doubt of a tree-climbing or low-flying predator when a dozen or more spears are pointed in their direction. The cacaphony of the rookery is enough to drive predators from the area quickly. There is not this early warning system available to solitary nesters.

Egg-turning is a crucial process, for the heat of the sitting bird must be radiated evenly throughout each egg. It is also necessary

OPPOSITE — *Nestlings tussle with each other to entertain themselves while their parents are off fishing.* Photo by Lynn M. Stone

FAMILY LIFE AND THE ROOKERY

to keep the embryo on the top side so full development can take place within the shell. Since egg-laying takes place in the inconsistent temperature of northern springs, in May, careful incubation is an ultimate concern of both birds. The incubation period takes 28 days.

We know from research what happens inside the shell, and it is magic. The egg is called the perfect "package" to carry something of value, and it is. The turning of the egg parents do regularly as the shifts of setting change. Meanwhile, the embryo feels the changes, even to the point of the head moving into what will be a workable position to break out.

There is a lining in the shell—notice this next when a hard boiled egg is shelled—and it is called the allantois. The embryo grows to the point when it will tear that film and then pip the shell. That tiny hole lets the first breath of air into the shell, causing the young bird to begin to use its lungs. The incoming air provides a newfound strength. About this time the bird's special "hatching muscle" and "egg tooth" being to work their single functions.

This is common to nearly all birds. The chick, still an embryo officially, braces its legs against the shell, just at the right upper point, and begins hammering away. Like a worker using a jackhammer, the little hatchling moves across the surface of the shell, gradually weakening its top. At the final moment, the shell breaks with the pounding of the special tooth, before the head and shoulders break through into the air.

A great blue clutch is hatched one at a time, mostly in the sequence of laying and could be a day apart, depending upon the

OPPOSITE — *Parents bring dinner in an easy-to-digest form to their young. Photo by Lynn M. Stone*

FAMILY LIFE AND THE ROOKERY

relative strength of the hatching muscle and the durability of the egg tooth. While this time frame might not seem consequential, that one day or two or three or four—depending on the size of the clutch— in the world of hatchling birds, literally starts the so-called pecking order. The bird who pecks through its shell first has the best chance of survival. At the end of the first year, only an estimated 31 percent of the first clutch will have survived starvation, predators like eagles, racoons, even bears, and falling out of the nest or starving within it. By the time the fledglings are ready to leave the nest, there are only two or three who have survived the initial ordeal.

Both parents respond to the new arrivals almost automatically. That means food. Throughout the hatching process, the embryo consumes nearly all the nutrients available within the perfect package. But when it arrives into the air, it must eat.

For the next six weeks or so, until the young birds can fly and find food on their own, the parents are responsible for their brood. Four days difference means that Egg #1 has actually consumed four times the food of Egg #4 when it opens its yawp. Defense and survival are keyed to that differential. However, it guarantees that at least a part of the clutch will be strong enough to survive.

It is at this point that the nest begins to become befouled with excess food and the nestlings' guano. The parents know their responsibility of food-gathering, so they go out, separately, to get as much as possible to keep their youngsters alive. Depending upon the environment, of course, and the quantity of food delivery, not its quality, the clutch will feed and grow. However, for people who want to see a nest, they will find, according to one

OPPOSITE — *Territory is territory -- that's what family is all about - so warnings are sometimes required for distant relations.*
Photo by Scott Nielsen

FAMILY LIFE AND THE ROOKERY

visitor "some fresh [food] and some in various stages of putrefaction." Seems that the young open mouths miss some of the regurgitated fish or frogs, and since odor is not a major consideration to the great blue, finding what was missed doesn't matter except to the hungriest of the brood.

What the great blue parents do comprehend, however, is when to begin to shut down the food supply. The typical picture of young beaks raised, everyone squawking "Me, first, me first!" is not unusual in the heron nest. The big difference is that the young herons' parents determine that there is a time when the kids are just shut off from "expected" meals. The great blue mother and father instinctively determine the point when the supply is going

ABOVE — *Sometimes territorial squabbles escalate to the level of physical confrontations.* Photo by Lynn M. Stone

FAMILY LIFE AND THE ROOKERY

to be less than the demand.

The parents resist the extensive protests, but the young herons are also gaining strength which they may not be aware of having. If there are the four young nestlings, plus one or two of the parents, they quickly begin to physically fill the nest with growing bodies. What began as a single male's nest is now chockablock with big and not very graceful or delicate birds.

Aesthetically even, there is none of the elegance in the young that will mark the heron as the one of the aristocrats of the bird kingdom. They are gangly creatures, mostly legs and neck. Their first feathers are a layer of silky, downy tufts, a sign of very immature feathers that are large quilled and contained within soft blue sheaths. Their legbones are so pliable that they will bend and not break—a feature of convenience in a crowded nest.

It only takes about four weeks before the slate-colored feathers begin to blossom. The bill has grown to a more traditional proportion relative to the head. The bones are now brittle, but the clumsy quartet becomes quite comical and as it tries to compete for space and feeding, it is often standing room only. The antics in the nest can have their tragic side, as occasionally one of the growing herons will be accidentally shoved out of the nest. Unable to fly, and perhaps breaking bones in the fall, it is likely that the chick will be then become a predator's dinner or just die from starvation or exposure at the base of the tree. On a bad day, perhaps after a violent wind storm, there might be a number of helpless, broken young birds on the ground.

While in their earliest days, the birds would be fed on each of

FAMILY LIFE AND THE ROOKERY

the parent's regurgitation shifts, once in the morning and once at dusk. Then the parents cut it to once a day, and then increase gaps between feedings. Expectantly, then comes the loudest hour of the rookery as dozens of young birds complain about the hunger they feel and call their parents to fill them up again. There is a lesson being learned, however, and that is that abstinence is not a desirable condition, that self-sustained subsistence is the desired status quo.

There comes a day when they are hungry enough to leap from the nest. In most cases, they discover they can suddenly fly. Once they experience that moment of mysterious realization, they jump into the feeding fray. This happens at about six to eight weeks after hatching. There are those ornithologists who believe that the rookery serves as an "information center" from which the birds determine the flight paths to food from returning great blues. There are those who feel there is no exchange of such information. However, it is possible that while the adults know where they are going for food, the young ones left behind do watch their parents and neighbors leave the nests and head off in a particular direction at certain times of the day.

From that point of initial flight, the self-dependent great blue is truly born. Instead of a hundred pairs, or a dozen pairs, out seeking food, though, there may be 600 or a thousand or more hungry birds looking for places to eat. It does not take long for that multiplication process to deplete existing resources, and that would explain why many adult birds continue on in their migration individually, flying to even further climes such as northern

FAMILY LIFE AND THE ROOKERY

Quebec, Nova Scotia, Alaska or Greenland to complete the summer feeding season.

The young learn quickly to find their own dinners. The seniority and superiority of hatching is not a condition of survival any longer. Whereas before the oldest in the nest ate the most and developed physically most rapidly, now it is cleverness of the surviving hatchlings that commands. The stronger might learn to fly farther, but the smarter learn to search out edibles in vacant places. The survival of the fittest continues to be the rule, but windows of opportunity begin to open to those who have that sixth sense of searching in the out-of-the-way spots. Now the competition for food that might still include the parents in the rookery's various nests causes the young fliers' range of exploration to be expanded, as they, too, gather strength for the late fall migration south.

Leaving Home

Those that survive that first long trip will usually make it through the first winter. The first trip is not easy, so losses do occur. Perhaps not enough energy has been generated to build the muscles and lungs and air sacs adequately for the initial long flight—there is no "storage" of food as within whales, for example. And the great blues fly night or day. So sometimes a storm will pull apart the siege, and a young one will become lost and never find its way. Herons, like other migrating birds, crash into power lines; they pick up diseases that weaken them; or they are shot on the wing or in roost along the way. But the vast majority of young great blues make the trip to wherever their grouping, which might include a variety of members of the heron family, has led them.

Audubon's study of the great blue about 150 years ago is still quite pertinent today, especially regarding the three-year maturation of the bird. He noted how the pendant crest starts in the first year, as does the filling out of the elongated feathers of the breast and shoulders that distinguish the great blue. The top of the head is pure white. And there is no breeding in the first year.

By the second spring, the maturing of the bird is recognizable, as the coloring of the upper feathers has gained the shading, and the black and white markings are almost complete. That exceptional crest now hangs over the back of the head three or

OPPOSITE — *Once out of the nest, the young bird is on its own when it comes to finding food. This unending quest begins less than two months after the bird is hatched.* Photo by Kim Harris

LEAVING HOME

four inches. While Audubon noticed that there might be some breeding done by the two-year-old male, it is limited, undoubtedly by the strength of the competing males. In the third spring, the great blue has earned its I.D. as a mature bird. It molts, is basically indistinguishable from other males or females, and has achieved its basic weight and height or wingspan.

By this time, the three-year-old has become totally conversant in great blue language. This has been variously described as *gronnk, graackk, quuuck, qua-qua, groark, pumpaugah, craaaok,* and *frahnk, frahnk, frawnk.* Roughly translated, but not necessarily in that sequence: "Hi, honey, I'm home." "Get out of here, stranger, or die." "Hey, mommy or daddy, I'm hungry." "Hey, buddy, you want to fight for her or not?" "It's my lake, mister." "Does anybody know where the flock went?" "Lousy fishing here, I'm moving on." Audubon calls them all "uncouth syllables," and that seems to fit the sound of the great blue. This is not a song bird, nor the lyrical loon. The great blue, a colonial loner, does not indulge in much conversation, save by way of warning, mostly.

One of the most interesting calls comes within the context of winter residence in southern waters. After flocking south, they separate to their instinctive, individualistic behavior. However, there are times when fish might shoal off a certain beach, and the great blues rendezvous via the heron "grapevine." Akin to the feeding frenzies of informal schools of sharks, the herons plunge into the shoal, ultimately with too many beaks and not enough fish. At some undefined point, however, there is a sudden call by the great blues. "Whoa, fellas, enough already!" In a moment, the

OPPOSITE — *A young great blue tries out its wings while still in the nest.* Photo by Lynn M. Stone

LEAVING HOME

OPPOSITE — *Now an adult, this great blue sports royal plumage and displays mature alertness.* Photo by Lynn M. Stone

ABOVE — *A young heron learns by watching its parents and other adult birds while in the nest, but will ultimately survive only on its own instincts and skills.* Photo by Scott Nielsen

FOLLOWING SPREAD — *All grown up.* Photo by Lynn M. Stone

130

LEAVING HOME

congregation backs off to their respective and respectful distances. One study has indicated that the "patience level" of a feeding heron is about four minutes, after which it either orders everybody else out of the pool or moves on.

Great blues live longer than most other species. Because of their elusive nature, and their inherent ability to fight against predators (including bird-banders), science has not established a truly compatible relationship that enables trackers to do extensive research on particular great blues. As with the loons, which have been around almost forever without providing the ornithologist much in the way of tracking certain patterns of migration or maturation or interlocution and breeding, data and research of the great blue is not much further from Audubon's mid-19th century conclusions.

How long do great blues live? Longer than turkeys or sparrow, not as long as eagles and condors. About 20 years, if the collected data is averaged. That is a fairly long time for a bird to fly, considering how many elements it must fight with each migration and each moment of competition for space and food. The great blue is a bird that is larger than life, for within that tall and lanky frame, surrounded by its great wingspan that is exceeded by few other birds, its body weight versus overall cubic dimensions indicate that it should probably not have made it through that mid-range of bird sizes and weights.

OPPOSITE — *Sometimes the great egret flies and feeds alongside the great blue heron.* Photo by Lynn M. Stone

The Great Blue's Future

It should be recognized that the great blue has undoubtedly survived the eons due to its particular defensive and survival characteristics, but recently laws forbidding their killing have helped greatly. The bird's beak, eye, feet, its solitary essence, and the amazing collaboration of instinctively hostile males and females in the mating and nesting process are all elements of success. It is also a good thing that the tradition of hunters to consider nestlings as easily acquired food has ended. Mankind might possibly have been the most dangerous predator, for unlike a racoon, man would refuse to be intimidated by irate parents in a quest for food, climbing a rookery tree. But it was easier to raise chickens than chase great blue nestlings, "Indian pullets," in a rookery.

Today, the greatest dangers to the great blue are environmental. While it is considered unlikely that this heron will go the way of the whooping crane or the passenger pigeon, we should be aware of the fact that this relatively ordinary pigeon went from four billion population to zero in fewer than 50 years. In the case of the passenger pigeon, of course, it was mass-hunting that wiped out the species. However, mankind is creating chemical equivalents of the great nets hunters hung to trap the pigeon and feed restaurant diners.

They speak of computer programs "crashing," being obliterated by unknown or obscure inputs. The various food

OPPOSITE — *Footprints in the sand are silent testimony to a quiet walk along the beach.* Photo by Robert McKenzie

THE GREAT BLUE'S FUTURE

"crashes" of frogs, certain fish, or even meadow mammals like mice or moles, can definitely affect the survival of the great blue and all other feeders on multiple resources. At least two things happen in a crash: one, a multitudinous portion of the food-chain disappears; two, in that disappearance, impregnated or contaminated inputs of the food-chain take place.

When the disappearance occurs, the food supply simply vanishes, as if by magic. When the experience occurs gradually, through contamination, the food-chain's mechanism of multiple ingestion continues. So, as the great blue continues to consume, for example, a species of frogs on the downslide due to chemical impregnation, there is an accumulative effect occurring that will be like feeding the bird arsenic in small doses. Eventually it will reach the dying point. Pollution of our natural environment tends to lead to the latter situation, as the food chain runs its link-by-link course according to the instincts and ignorance of nature.

There is no end in sight to the ability of mankind to slowly, or quickly, close the pages of the chapters on the lifespan of our fellow creatures. We tend to gather our greed in a collective spurt of energy and try to achieve wealth of one kind or another. Those motivated by such desires are the last ones to care for the sustenance of species so obscure—whales, great blue herons, horned owls, wolves—that ignorance of them covers concern for the future of a full Earth.

No doubt, evolution is coded into the futures of all creatures and death is the eventuality of all species. But the great blue heron will stand a sentinel over all its fellow creatures for many

OPPOSITE — *It takes three years for a great blue to fully mature.*
Photo by Scott Nielsen

THE GREAT BLUE'S FUTURE

more eons. It is too swift to be taken by stealth, only by the stupidity of a human hunter. It is too lean to be considered a good meal. It is too beautiful to be considered extraneous.

There is, however, in addition to chemical pollutants that might endanger the great blue's survival, the threat to habitats by curious, nature-loving human beings. As we come to appreciate our natural surroundings and environment, more of us flock to parks and refuges to witness our fellow inhabitants bound by gravity to the earth. Our own numbers are beginning to create problems.

There is no more dramatic example than that of Florida's Sanibel Island's J.N."Ding" Darling National Wildlife Refuge. The 5,000 acre refuge was created as a safe haven for about 300 species of birds and other creatures. It was also created in the spirit of "ecotourism," that new phenomenon of people going to someplace other than a zoo to see protected wildlife, flora and fauna.

Sanibel's year-round population hovers around 5,800, but in 1989 more than three million eco-tourists dropped by to see life in the refuge. It wasn't enough that Florida and the island were caught in a drought that was shrinking the feeding grounds for the birds, including great blues, ibises and spoonbills, which was driving the bird population inland and into more concentrated areas. Now there were three million humans polluting the air with the petroleum fumes of their cars, with the mountains of trash left behind, and the increased volume of noise throughout most of the day. The shallow sloughs and the seashore were often filled with so many people, canoeing or picnicking and swimming, that the spots where waders would normally feed were off-limits.

OPPOSITE — *Sunset shadows cloak a great blue.* Photo by Stephen Kirkpatrick

THE GREAT BLUE'S FUTURE

"The people treat Sanibel as if they were at the zoo," one ranger said. Graduate students are writing papers with titles like "The Effects of High-level Human Visitation on Foraging Water Birds." And there is talk of setting vehicular limits, charging high fees to enter the refuge, and increasing the policing of eco-tourist behavior and activities. In Delaware's Prime Hook National Wildlife Refuge and the Trap Pond State Park, canoeists and hikers become the summertime companions of great blues foraging in the warm shallows of the sea or the inland ponds and waterways. So far the eco-tourist numbers have stayed reasonably small as to avoid the problems of the J.N. "Ding" Darling National Wildlife Refuge, but the potential threat is always driving down the highway looking for something to see or do over a long weekend or short vacation.

Wading bird studies are being constantly conducted across the country. They are, for example, "the most obvious vertebrate components of the Okefenokee Swamp ecosystem," writes Deborah Boring of the University of Georgia. Most have heard of the fabled Okefenokee found in southeastern Georgia, a "primeval blackwater wetland," but few comprehend its significance to a portion of the South's colonial wading bird population. In one small area Boring studied, Macks Island, 200 acres provided habitat for anywhere between 10,000 and 30,000 wading birds, mostly white ibises but also a significant variety of herons. Her study focussed on the two different swamp habitats that were involved between the feeding areas and the transportation of nutrients and energy resources to the rookeries.

Jean-Luc DesGranges of the Canadian Wildlife Service worked with

---

PRECEDING SPREAD — *Looking back over the past.* Photo by *Stephen Kirkpatrick*

OPPOSITE — *A heritage of millions of years, embodied in a beautiful creature standing silent and motionless.* Photo by *Dusty Perin*

STORIES OF THE GREAT BLUE

the great blue colonies of Quebec's Gaspe area, specifically concerned with flight patterns and feeding areas. "Coloniality developed because it facilitates the location of food," he says, revealing that he is one of those who believes that the heronry serves as an information center. He points to the fact that the direction taken by the birds is not a random decision. Some go out the way they entered, while others follow the flightline of ones that have left the rookery and still others take off in a completely different direction than they or others have used. Departure is generally triggered by "predictable environmental changes," such as tide fluctuations, sunset or sunrise. DesGranges also points to the evidence that the larger the colony the greater number of birds fledged per nest because of the increased defense capacity and the greater food resources.

One Canadian study worked with 61 colonies that had almost 3,500 breeding pairs of great blues. Another in Ohio focused on the activities of 1,000 nests in three rookeries. This particular Toledo-area study had a certain humorous "futility of science" dimension. The ornithologist wanted to capture some great blues so they could be banded and have radio transmitters attached. The scientist's team tried several methods over about a two-year period: snare carpets were laid in the shallow waters where the great blue heron fed, but failed to snag their feet; almost invisible "mist" nets were hung in the flying paths and the loafing areas, but the birds avoided them; night lighting was tried, but the birds weren't fazed. All methods were unsuccessful.

Finally, the scientists used rocket nets, employing three ten-pound rockets that propelled 1,800 square feet of 2" mesh netting

PRECEDING SPREAD — *Looking toward the future.* Photo by *Lynn M. Stone*

STORIES OF THE GREAT BLUE

into the air above a feeding heron. Eleven attempts caught eight great blues. Within ten minutes they were banded, fitted with radio transmitters, and allowed to fly away. No mortality—to bird or scientist—occurred, or injury. However, the results of the project are also as out of reach as the herons captured.

The work of science is closeted — not just for great blues but loons and grey whales and others — by the fact that migratory creatures are not cooperative by nature. They change their patterns, their feeding grounds, their rookeries, nests and annual mates. Merely mortal human beings will continue to haunt the multitude of habitats and environs looking for answers to the myriad questions developed in the classroom, the field, and the laboratory. Most likely, we will continue the trade-off of curiosity and ignorance, being kept in the dark by those creatures we find most mysterious because we are not concerned by their relative obscurity.

Stories Of The Great Blue

We can bring the Great Blue Heron closer to us, into the epochs of human history. We can say that these records are in the category of sanctity or of sacred places. We do not know for certain, for they might just be renditions of favorite moments in an individual's life.

Two admirable images come to mind. One is a mural on the wall of an ancient Egyptian tomb, still vivid and illustrative 2,500 years after its painting. The other is found on a span of stone on the shore of a lake in Ontario, Canada, and might be almost as old, as a crooked-neck heron flies on a wall alongside the universal Thunderbird, the turtle, and men.

The 15th Century B.C. Egyptian mural is heralded in its book as being a paean to the sacredness of pintail ducks in a papyrus marsh. While it is true that there are about a half-dozen pintails on the whitewashed walls of the tomb and are considered "minor Egyptian gods," a more homely interpretation is deserved: not everything is holy in the official, spiritual sense.

Let us consider the mural. We don't know if the man buried there loved duckhunting, but the fact that two of the flying birds are cleverly brought down by a kind of crooked wood, almost a

OPPOSITE — *Silhouetted against the shades of dusk, a great blue roosts for the night.* Photo by Scott Nielsen

STORIES OF THE GREAT BLUE

boomerang, indicates that somebody knew about Egyptian duckhunting. The mural shows pintails, but also at least one mallard and a female, watching a nest with two eggs, as does one male.

Most fascinating is the bird in the lower left corner of the mural, for there, neck crooked and wings wide in flight, is a blue heron. There is no mistaking that curved neck that separates the heron from the crane. There is no way to ignore the blue coloring of the wide wingspread and head. There is no way to translate its real meaning, regardless of one book's interpretation of the heron's presence as being a "decoy."

Let us hazard a guess at one of this antique Egyptian leader's life's joys. He enjoyed going out into the papyrus marshes of the sidewaters of the Nile, that great green stripe of life that feeds the people of the desert sands in that part of the world.

This man is a hunter. He and his slaves knew how to throw the snake-headed, curved sticks from their blinds, at exactly the right time of flight to hit the ducks in their necks and bring them down. Perhaps the representation of the heron is that of a decoy, but perhaps not. Decoys and "scarecrows" have been used for thousands of years, but let us consider an alternative accorded to the long-dead Egyptian hunter and his love of the marshes and lakes of his kingdom.

There is no way to know, but those who have either fished, hunted or just paddled their way through lowland waters know the singular beauty of the heron. Even if we agree that all the designs in the Egyptian mural are symbolic, have deep religious meaning - and that might be what the family desired - in our heart of hearts,

OPPOSITE — *During a long hunt for prey, a heron gives one leg a rest while remaining motionless in the water.* Photo by Scott Nielsen

STORIES OF THE GREAT BLUE

ABOVE — *It takes only a few feet and not much wing movement for a great blue heron to get airborne. Photo by Stephen Kirkpatrick*

STORIES OF THE GREAT BLUE

some of us might hazard that this is one scene that the departed did not want to forget even in the long passage into the unknown. Let him hunt pintails in the autumn among the papyrus and recall that isolated sentinel who would take to wing as the ducks were in flight and being brought down.

Knowing the range of the great blue to be only in the Western Hemisphere, we must hazard a guess as to the kind of heron our hunter in antiquity admired. Being an African heron, it might be the *ardea godiath*, the goliath heron, largest of the global family. Yet that bird has a chestnut-colored head and its body plumage is definitely black and white. There is the purple heron that still ranges in the Egyptian marshes, but that is also chestnut and has black and white stripes. Perhaps in those days long ago, the European grey heron ranged that far south across the Mediterranean, but it has no colors that come close to bluish. So what could it be? If it is not a brightly colored, painted decoy, it might have been a little egret which has a blue-grey coloring and does inhabit the vicinity of the Red Sea. We will never know for sure, but the hunter who loved pintails and the papyrus marshes knew.

Half a world away, on the shores of the Great Lakes and their various glacially fed and linked waters, we have the American aboriginal people. They do not hunt for sport, for they must survive long winters and short summers. Yet, they, too, have their artists and recorders of lifestyles of the time.

It might have been the same basic temporal frame, for we do not know if these etchings were made 500 or 2,000 years ago. In a remarkable Canadian book, *Indian Rock Paintings of the Great*

STORIES OF THE GREAT BLUE

Lakes, the explorer-anthropologist Selwyn Dewdney found only two ornithological etchings—other than the omnipresent Thunderbird— and they were both great blue herons.

How do we know? Since they did not use colored inks or paints as in Egypt, we can only go by contemporary migratory patterns and that classic curved neck that separates the crane from the heron. Dewdney might call one representation that of "a clumsy heron," but it still was the only water fowl that the original folks of the area thought about drawing on stone with dust and paint and charcoal sticks.

Adding to the meaning of the drawings of our first residents is the simple fact that the rock paintings are found on what we would consider cliff faces. Hardly the habitat of the great blue itself, but let us recall Dewdney's own diary entries: "It was a joy to have an Indian in the bow—an unusually good canoeman... I was lucky to have him along, for most of the site was exposed to the waves and we had a wild time taking tracings..."

Let us imagine a pair or quartet of native American hunters or fishermen following the coastline, looking for a safe, calm refuge from high water and wind-driven waves. If one were the tribal artist, he would record the journey, the history, as well as the invocations of the threatened men.

So the Thunderbird, the sacred symbol of rebirth, is painted on the ledges. So are germane moments of these early voyagers, showing simple representations of the number in the canoes, the sun and moon, snakes and arrows. Then comes the heron, a memory perhaps of quieter times at home, along soft shores and

---

OPPOSITE — *A rookery penthouse suite. Photo by Robert W. Baldwin*

STORIES OF THE GREAT BLUE

quiet creeks, where the watchful sentinel, steel grey and softly feathered seemed to watch over the family, the grouping. Who would first fly at the need of alarm? The heron. Who would sense strangers even before the human eye or ear could see or hear them? The heron. Who would return, solitary and wise, each year, stay and stand almost as tall as a man? The great blue heron.

Dewdney and Kenneth Kidd document their discoveries of hundreds of rock paintings of the upper Great Lakes. Henry Schoolcraft, one of the nation's first "live-in" anthropologists, spending most of his life among the Great Lakes Chippewa/ Ojibwa/Anishinabe people, found the pictographs of the heron and hardly distinguishes that bird from the one that has been called the "Crane Clan" in generations of Ojibwa/Anishinabe. In fact, it is demonstrated graphically in the Anishinabe illustrations that accompany renegotiations of an 1842 treaty.

We have the fish and animal clans represented, with their various links to Anishinabe bands living in the Wisconsin Territory, and there is a great blue, long-legged, long-necked, crested and standing bird. From the crest, where the several feathers flow are lines that link the bird with the other animal-fish clans of the people.

The bird is as blue as the Wisconsin River and the several lakes that accompany the figures of other colors. It is, it must be, a great blue heron, a definite native to the region and standing taller than the beaver, the rabbit, and the walleye. Audubon noted that folks called the great blue a "blue crane" and a "crane," so it is not unlikely that the translators from Schoolcraft onward would apply their own standards to the words; but there is no mistaking the

STORIES OF THE GREAT BLUE

ABOVE — *The little blue heron does not grow up to be a great blue, but it does colorfully live up to its name.* Photo by Kim Harris

STORIES OF THE GREAT BLUE

blueness of that official bird in the new treaty of 1849.

It is interesting to push our imaginations to wonder about the various traits of the great blue heron that separate it from other birds that might be considered equally significant if not relatively numerous. But to elevate the bird to a ranking of spiritual and cultural importance is to give it the meaning that each of us must feel as we see the solitary great blue standing absolutely still, elegant and imperious, charismatic and silent, a being truly deserving of our attention and reverence.

One final story, that brings in the culture of the remote Solomon Islands. Children there are given a story that might be considered a South Pacific equivalent to one of "Aesop's Fables." They hear the tale of "The Heron and the Turtle" and it can serve as both a reminder of the bird's range and its different environments and feeding grounds. We are most likely considering the tiger heron as the central character, it should be noted.

It is a meaningful story because it involves creatures as being potential victims of nature and other consumers. Usually the Solomon Islanders begin with words like, "The slender and graceful heron was fishing one day..." The children learn how the lithe neck and the powerful, spear-like beak lashes out and catches its dinner of fish.

Then a problem for all creatures of tidal basins and flows, in the South Pacific or the Gulf of Mexico or the waters of Florida: When the tides move, creatures cannot afford to be trapped. Often it is a race against moon time, and the waters drain out or flow in at great speeds.

In this story, a heron is stalking fish in the shallow coral pools.

OPPOSITE — *Encroaching darkness does not stop the never-ending quest for food.* Photo by Stephen Kirkpatrick

STORIES OF THE GREAT BLUE

He recognizes the acceleration of the tide and ambles shoreward. Suddenly, his foot is caught in one of the oblique angles of coral that surrounds the island environment.

No matter how much he twists and turns, the four-toed foot will not release as the water creeps up the heron's legs. Birds have lungs so they worry about the availability of air. Trapping by the tide is terror to all creatures dependent upon breathing, and the heron fights against time.

The tale has the heron pleading with the shark, the biola fish, the garfish, the crocodile for help. All of them say, "I'm too busy just now..." as the water rises about the heron's beak.

Finally, a turtle swims close by the heron. Out goes the plea, in comes the admission, "Well, perhaps I can help, but what will I gain?"

The heron, with its sharp eye for food, tells the turtle that a sea urchin is running the coral rock beneath his eyes. So he promises a nice dinner to the turtle. Thank you, invitation accepted.

The turtle eats the urchin and then stays below the tide to free the foot of the heron. "As the water closes over the head of the normally calm bird, the turtle releases its foot from the coral trap," the tale reads.

Naturally, the nearly-drowned heron, a non-diving bird, is full of gratuity. "I shall remember your goodness to me all my life, and if there is anything to help you, I promise I will do it."

Tales have a universal application, so it is not unexpected that the turtle finds itself a victim of another kind of trap, nets set out by fishermen, who won't deal with the shark, or the other creatures from which the heron sought to gain help. Human excuses range from danger to "too many bones" to luck. They like

STORIES OF THE GREAT BLUE

ABOVE — *The green-backed heron wears its color well, and its crooked neck proves the family connection.* Photo by Stephen Kirkpatrick

STORIES OF THE GREAT BLUE

the thought of turtle soup and suppers.

The trapped turtle finally connects with the heron that had vowed to help. The tale takes particular affection in the ability of the heron to uproot the trap that has caught the turtle. A very complex song sequence is set up by the heron, involving the enthrallment of the people of the village, during which the turtle is being told which stakes to pull up from the trap.

"The Dancing Heron" brings in a variety of cultural aspects, all of which are keyed to actions the turtle must take to free itself.

The tale ends with a sort of kind composure by the heron, a gracious fatigue:

> "Now that it is all over,
> Now that it is finished,
> My dance is ended,
> How did you like it?"

And then the heron flies away toward the setting sun across the horizon. At that time, the fisherpeople discover that maybe there is a problem in the water of the coral reef but they never know they have been fooled. There is just no turtle in the trap. Instead, the people scratch their heads, and there is a heron walking the ridges of living stone, while beneath the surface, out of their sight, is a turtle cooling itself in clear water.

While we might have to go far afield or retreat to antiquity to find memorable tales about the great blue heron, there is no mistaking its indelible identity within our imaginations. How many inns or supper clubs in more remote areas (like Mercer, Wisconsin), have places called The Blue Heron? Or resorts and motels?

In Hammondsport, New York, within the fabled Finger Lakes

OPPOSITE — *For great blue herons, calling out invitations and strutting one's stuff is all part of the ritual mating dance.* Photo by Scott Nielsen

STORIES OF THE GREAT BLUE

area, there is a winery called Heron Hill. There is no mistaking the great blue flying over a vineyard that is the central figure on the labels of the variety of wine bottled at Heron Hill Winery. There is even a rock-and-roll group travelling America's Heartland called "Mud Claw and the Blue Herons." Perhaps honoring the travelling nature of this wonderful wading bird, motorists heading west on the Ohio Turnpike will find symbolic the presence of the Blue Heron Plaza between Cleveland and Toledo. The great blue heron appears in many forms, in many places.

STORIES OF THE GREAT BLUE

ABOVE — *Each year the great blue heron enjoys the "fully-feathered look" for the mating season, then molting begins.* Photo *by Scott Nielsen*

STORIES OF THE GREAT BLUE

OPPOSITE — *At times, even the great blue heron gets its feathers ruffled.* Photo by Bill Marchel

ABOVE — *One blackbird does not make a mob, but here one attempts to discourage a great blue on its hunt, which could include the blackbird's own nestlings.* Photo by Scott Nielsen

STORIES OF THE GREAT BLUE

ABOVE — *Egrets and herons have learned to share feeding waters.* Photo by Stephen Kirkpatrick

OPPOSITE — *The great blue looks radiant in its finery, but its voice does not inspire concertos as do those of the cardinal and the cuckoo.* Photo by Scott Nielsen

STORIES OF THE GREAT BLUE

PRECEDING SPREAD — *Landing in the marshlands.*
Photo by Stephen Kirkpatrick

ABOVE — *Standing room only in the rookery.* *Photo by
Dusty Perin*

OPPOSITE — *Eyes forward, beak level, the great blue
can be aloft at the slightest hint of perceived danger.*
Photo by Scott Nielsen

ABOUT THE AUTHOR

Hayward Allen is the third generation of Allen writer/editors. "My grandfather began as a typesetter and built the Sioux City Journal a century ago, and my father worked as a reporter in Tennessee and Ohio, so I seem to come by a keyboard genetically," Hayward says. Born in Tennessee, raised in places like Virginia, Hawaii, California, Ohio, and a graduate of the University of Colorado, Hayward joined the Peace Corps in 1962 and was given a teaching assignment at a teacher training institute in Harar, Ethiopia.

"The Peace Corps was my real education," he said. "Colorado may have given me a BA, MA and teaching certificate, but Ethiopia truly opened my eyes to what life was basically about. After my experience in eastern Africa, it was impossible to look at any environment with those youthful, naive eyes."

After travelling through several north African and near-Eastern countries, Hayward settled in Venice, Italy, "to write the definitive expatriate American novel." The manuscript found its way into the slow Venetian canals at the stroke of the New Year 1965. That's the symbolic moment when various parts of one's past are discarded and the novel joined a flowage of broken dolls, at least one artificial leg, empty wine casks, and other miscellaneous items that would float. Breakable things simply went out the windows. . ."

ABOUT THE AUTHOR

After working as an editor and writer for a London "gentleman's" magazine, Hayward returned to the United States as a doctoral candidate at the University of New York-Buffalo. "Leslie Fiedler was there, as well as John Barth, Charles Olson and Robert Creeley, and together they formed a kind of quartet of contemporary American writing," Hayward remembers. He taught freshman composition and studied for two years before being offered a teaching job at the University of Wisconsin-Oshkosh.

"Married and a father, I could not see myself living the ascetic life of a teaching assistant until my son was in high school," he recalls. "So we went to Wisconsin. I have never regretted the move."

Over the subsequent years, Hayward has written for a wide variety of publications, as artscritic, movie and drama reviewer, editor of broadcasting publications, writer of environmental and security articles, manager of corporate communications, and working as a specialist in international and cooperative relations. "Finding NorthWord Press was, I believe, a very serendipitous connection. For years, I have watched and wondered about the wonderful variety of creatures in our woods and fields," he says.

These days find Hayward Allen, now father of three grown adults and married to Ronda Lyon Allen, who works for the Wisconsin Division of Tourism, working on various writing projects that range from corporate environmentalism to investigations of different species that consider Wisconsin home for at least part of the year. "There are those writers who are content to stay within a narrow line of fences," he says, "but my interests move across a broad horizon."

Sources

Among the books consulted in the writing of The Great Blue Heron are the following:

Audubon, James. *Birds of North America*, edited by Dean Amadon, 1967.

Burton, Richard. *Bird Behavior*, Knopf, New York, 1985.

Dorst, Jean. *The Life of Birds*, translated by I.C.J. Galbraith, Columbia University Press, New York, 1974.

. *Migration of Birds*, Houghton Mifflin, New York, 1962.

Eckert, Alan W. *The Wading Birds of North America*, illustrated by Karl E. Karalus, Weathervane Books, New York, 1981.

Hancock, James, and James Kushlar. *The Herons Handbook*, illustrated by Robert Gillmor and Peter Hayman, Harper and Row, New York, 1984.

Hossenbach, Hans. *Family Life of Birds*, McGraw Hill, New York, 1971.

Hochbaum, Albert. *Travels and Traditions of Waterfowl*, University of Minnesota Press, 1965.

Lawrence, Susannah. *The Audubon Society Field Guide to the Natural Places of the Mid-Atlantic: Coastal*, Pantheon Books, New York, 1984.

Matthiessen, Peter. *Wildlife in North America*, Viking, New York, 1959.

Nethersole-Thompson, Desmond & Maimie. *Waders: Their Breeding, Haunts, and Watchers*, T. and A.D. Poyser, Great Britain, 1986.

Perrins, C.M. *Avian Ecology*, Blackie (UK)/Chapman and Hall (NY), 1983.

Peters, James Lee. *Birds of the World*, 15 Volumes, Harvard University Press, 1934.

Robbins, Chandler S. and Bertel Brunn, Herbert S. Zim. *Guide to Field Identification: Birds of North America*, Golden Press, New York, 1966.

Peterson, Roger Tory. *A Field Guide to the Birds: Eastern Land and Water Birds*, Houghton Mifflin, New York, 1947.

. *The Birds, Time Life Books*, New York, 1973.

Soothill, Eric & Richard. *Wading Birds of the World*, Blandford Press, Great Britian, 1982.

Welty, Joel Carl. *The Life of Birds*, Knopf, New York, 1972.

Birds in Our Lives, edited by Alfred Stefferud, U.S. Department of Interior, 1966-1971.

Catalogue of Birds of the Americas, Field Museum of Natural History, 11 Volumes, Chicago, 1942.

*The Encylopedia of Bird*s, edited by Christopher M. Perrins and Alex L.A. Middleton, Facts on File Publications, New York, 1985.

Habitat Selection in Birds, edited by Martin L. Cody, Academic Press, New York, 1985.

Among the periodicals consulted are the following:

"American Way"

"Canadian Field Naturalist"

"Journal of Wildlife Management"

"Living Bird"

"New York Times"

"Oikos"

"Proceedings of the North American Wildlife Conference"

"Proceedings of the Colonial Waterbird Group"

"Wilson Bulletin"

"Wildbird"

Also From NorthWord